Group
Work With
Children and
Adolescents

SAGE SOURCEBOOKS FOR THE HUMAN SERVICES SERIES

Series Editors: ARMAND LAUFFER and CHARLES GARVIN

Recent Volumes in This Series

Group Work With Children and Adolescents

Prevention and Intervention in School and Community Systems

Sage Sourcebooks for
the Human Services

SIS|+|S

MACKEY LIBRARY
Trevecca Nazarene University

Steven R. Rose

SAGE Publications
International Educational and Professional Publisher
Thousand Oaks London New Delhi

For information:

SAGE Publications, Inc.
2455 Teller Road
Thousand Oaks, California 91320
E-mail: order@sagepub.com

SAGE Publications Ltd.
6 Bonhill Street
London EC2A 4PU
United Kingdom

SAGE Publications India Pvt. Ltd.
M-32 Market
Greater Kailash I
New Delhi 110 048 India

Printed in the United States of America

Library of Congress Cataloging-in-Publication Data

Rose, Steven R.
  Group work with children and adolescents: Prevention and
intervention in school and community systems / by Steven R. Rose.
    p. cm. -- (Sage sourcebooks for the human services; vol. 38)
  Includes bibliographical references and index.
  ISBN 0-7619-0160-4 (cloth : acid-free paper)
  ISBN 0-7619-0161-2 (pbk. : acid-free paper)
  1. Social work with teenagers. 2. Social work with children. 3.
Social group work. 4. School social work. I. Title. II. Series:
Sage sourcebooks for the human services series.
  HV1421 .R67 1998
  362.7'1—ddc21   98-9035

This book is printed on acid-free paper.

98 99 00 01 02 03 04 10 9 8 7 6 5 4 3 2 1

Acquisition Editor:	Jim Nageotte
Editorial Assistant:	Heidi Van Middlesworth
Production Editor:	Wendy Westgate
Editorial Assistant:	Denise Santoyo
Typesetter/Designer:	Rose Tylak
Indexer:	Virgil Diodato

CONTENTS

Part II: Applications of Group Work

PREFACE

Many of the social problems of children and adolescents are amenable to prevention or intervention through group work. Children and adolescents are prone to develop a wide range of social problems in family and peer relationships, social competence, mental health, substance abuse, and school performance. With reductions in support available in many family relationships, peer relationships have become increasingly important to many children and adolescents.

Acceptance by and participation in peer groups, which are highly valued by most children and adolescents, tend to provide the youngsters with opportunities for furthering their social development. Nevertheless, some youngsters lack such opportunities. Withdrawn and aggressive children and adolescents who are neglected, isolated, or rejected by their peers, can benefit from group work that is designed to develop their social competencies.

Although many children and adolescents remain in the same schools and communities from one year to the next, some have the experience of entering new ones. Transitions between schools and between communities, which include normative transfers and graduations as well as extraordinary events, such as changes in geographical location due to family disruption, tend to increase the stressors experienced by young people. Children and adolescents who change schools and communities often have more situations and persons to adjust to, and have a greater likelihood of developing interpersonal and social problems than young-sters in more stable situations. Children and adolescents who are highly stressed may benefit from acquiring coping skills in group work.

OUTLINE OF THE BOOK

The first part of the book presents concepts of a problem-solving approach to group work. Chapter 1 describes the social and environ-mental context of group work with children and adolescents. It provides the rationale and context, as well as the advantages and limitations, of group work. Chapter 2 explicates the problem-solving approach to group work, which reflects stressors experienced by and thought pro-cesses of members.

Chapter 3 describes the use of planning, composition, and assessment to form effective groups. Preventive and interventive processes and the uses of several types of activities are presented. The developmental phases of problem-solving group work are described, along with prac-tice guidelines.

Chapter 4 contains the purposes and types of evaluation of group work with children and adolescents. Suggestions for conducting evalu-ations in school and community systems are provided.

Chapter 5 reviews research on the effectiveness of group work with children and adolescents. The chapter reconsiders the problem-solving approach to group work, its applications in and relationship to school and community systems, as well as emerging social issues for school-age children and adolescents.

The second part of the book focuses on applications of the problem-solving approach to group work. Each chapter presents the purpose, rationale, and advantages of group work for dealing with a particular social problem. Ideas for practice include assessment, problem recog-nition, planning and composition, leadership, and activities. An exam-ple of a group is provided for each social problem.

Chapter 6 discusses group work with children and adolescents from families in which separation and divorce have occurred. Such group work practice is widely used to help the many youngsters who are affected by divorce.

Chapter 7 examines group work to improve peer relationships and social competence. The chapter emphasizes the use of interpersonal-cognitive problem-solving skills in developing friendships.

Chapter 8 describes the use of group work with children and adolescents who are at risk for developing mental health and substance abuse disorders. Such disorders, whose recognition was once limited to adults, are now more commonly recognized among children and adolescents.

Group work aimed at increasing the achievement levels of children and adolescents with academic problems is considered in Chapter 9. Truancy and dropout prevention are among the problems included in the school performance chapter.

ACKNOWLEDGMENTS

I thank Charles Garvin for his ample editorial contributions to this work, ranging from conception to implementation. His exemplary vision of group work with children and adolescents is reflected throughout this book.

My heartfelt gratitude is expressed to the editorial staff at Sage. Jim Nageotte is a superlative editor. His recommendations were astute, adroit, and timely. I also gladly acknowledge the efficient work of Heidi Van Middlesworth, Ellen R. Girden, and Wendy Westgate.

I wish to thank my colleagues at Louisiana State University for their support of my work. Kenneth Diehl, Lyn Louden, Shannon Robshaw, Cynthia M. Steed, and Lisa M. Theriot provided diligent assistance in carrying out part of the ground work for this book.

I express my appreciation to Ken Millar of Louisiana State University and Alan York of Bar-Ilan University for their sponsorship of the sabbatical during which substantial portions of this book were written.

Thanks are also due to the staff of the Louisiana State University, Bar-Ilan University, and Hebrew University of Jerusalem libraries, and the Central Library for Social Work in Jerusalem.

Finally, I thank my wonderful family, whose sustenance has been an essential element of authoring this book.

PART I

CONCEPTS OF GROUP WORK

Chapter 1

THE CONTEXT OF PRACTICE

The purpose of this chapter is to provide a broad view of group work with children and adolescents in school and community systems. The context of group work will be presented from ecological and social systems, community and social problems, educational, and organizational perspectives.

MULTIPLE PERSPECTIVES

Ecological and Social Systems Perspectives

The ecological perspective encompasses the interrelationship of social systems ranging from individual children to society as a whole and transactions between and within such systems (Brown & Swanson, 1988). Children and adolescents are in constant transaction with multiple social systems, including their families, peers, schools, communities, and the wider society.

Children tend to be very involved with their families. Family problems, including marital conflict and divorce, underlie much group work practice with children and adolescents (see Chapter 6). Of course, as children develop into adolescents, their transactions with social systems tend to become wider and more extensive. As a youngster, Henry played exclusively with children in the same building of the metropolitan housing development in which he lived. Nonetheless, when he got older Henry spent more time out of the building and in the far reaches of the housing development, away from the watchful eyes of his concerned

3

mother. There he met with other adolescents from the development who discussed their lives as they traded sex, drugs, music, and stolen goods. Eventually, their haven was discovered by a police officer, who brought in a social worker to meet with them.

The ecological perspective focuses on the relationship between youngsters and their environments, the stressors they experience, and the mechanisms they employ to cope with anxiety (Germain, 1988). The socioecological perspective, a variant of the ecological perspective, is rooted in systems theory and assumes that dysfunctional role performance is a product of a misalignment between the needs of children and adolescents and available environmental resources (Freeman, 1985). Potential members include youngsters whose psychosocial needs have not been adequately met through their extant social systems. A satisfactory match between the characteristics, requirements, resources, competencies, and cultures of children and adolescents with their environments increases the likelihood that they will function adequately. Accordingly, children and adolescents who have unsatisfactory relationships with their environments are likely to experience considerable stress. Such difficulties have been noted in group work with Hispanic and Asian adolescent immigrants (Glasgow & Gouse-Sheese, 1995; Lopez, 1991; Tannenbaum, 1990).

Unfortunately, a mismatch often exists between the program characteristics of junior high, intermediate, and middle schools and the developmental characteristics of young or early adolescents (Eccles & Midgley, 1989). Indeed, such middle-grade schools often aggravate the problems of adolescents (Carnegie Task Force on Education of Young Adolescents, 1989). George's parents received numerous complaints about their son's conduct at school. In earlier years, George had been described by his teachers as a good child. Nonetheless, in seventh grade he was constantly in trouble. In the latest report he was described as having kicked in a boy's briefcase. His parents were puzzled about the change in him, as everything seemed to be the same in the family. Nonetheless, some of the stressors at his new school, including frequent class changes during the day, were contributing to his difficulties. The school social worker considered George to be a good candidate for group work.

The social systems model provides a frame of reference for understanding the dynamics and interrelationships of social groups. Community and school systems consist of both large and small social groups with differing dynamics. Whereas large groups tend to be more task oriented, small groups tend to be more supportive. Nurit tended to feel lost in her large urban high school, composed of 9,000 students. Nonetheless, she felt much better when she participated in a small chorus at school.

Children and adolescents are likely to experience fewer social problems when value agreement exists between social systems. Group work has revealed cultural degradation experienced by Caribbean adolescents in North America (Glasgow & Gouse-Sheese, 1995). Group work with Hispanic adolescents has been useful in increasing awareness of cultural differences (Lopez, 1991). Furthermore, group work with Vietnamese adolescents has helped resolve members' conflicts between old (Vietnamese) and new (American) cultures. Anne's family came from a small island nation off the coast of Africa. Owing to her religious beliefs, when children in her class observed Christmas, Anne was unable to join them in their holiday meal. As the children misunderstood her beliefs, they expected her to participate. Anne felt different, lonely, and isolated. A social worker inaugurated a group work project to increase cross-cultural understanding between school children.

As systems, groups are composed of interacting and interdependent components and have boundaries that mark their limits, define internal and external aspects, separate them from systems, and protect them from environmental stressors (Pollak & Schaffer, 1984). For optimal functioning, groups exchange information with their environment and have clear boundaries. In some school and community systems, a strong demarcation between the group and the environment is established as in alternative programs within mainstream high schools. To maintain group boundaries, two types of contracts or agreements usually are established. Inside contracts, which are formed between members, specify the rules about exchange of information with persons outside the group. For instance, the members agreed to limit discussions with nonmembers to the general content and direction of a community group. To shield members from conflicting demands and expectations, outside contracts are formed between leaders and administrators. For instance, a school principal agreed that during the school day the members could spend time in the group rather than in their classroom curriculum area.

Community and Social Problems Perspectives

Schools and communities vary to the extent that they have children and adolescents with special education, poverty, and minority population concentrations. Community characteristics that are used to determine staffing levels for social services to children and adolescents include population (size, socioeconomic status), resources (public or private, level of services available), lack of resources, rural or urban or suburban, mobility of population (degree of transiency), unemployment rate, and incidence of single-parent families (National Council of State Consultants for School Social Work Services, 1981).

Some school and community systems are beset with family, mental health, and performance problems. The demand for multipurpose group work in high schools is directly related to the preponderance of social problems (Berkovitz, 1975). When the entire school system has significant problems, the system itself is sometimes a target of change. In a medium-size New England community, it was well known that Aboula High School was beset with high rates of teen pregnancy, crime, and dropouts. In addition to initiating a program of group work for the students, social workers began to work with the families, churches, and community organizations in an attempt to reduce the difficulties of the adolescents.

Changes in the sociodemographic characteristics of school and community populations may exacerbate tensions between children and adolescents who are members of diverse cultural groups. Group work can promote intercultural interaction as occurred in a middle school program for Latino, black, white, and Asian students (Bilides, 1990). At a middle school cafeteria, three white students threw eggs at Nicole and Talithea, who were shocked and stunned. Word spread about the incident, which sparked an uproar at school. As the pupil-personnel-service team could not contain the tensions engendered by the incident, the assistant principal called in the police, who responded quickly.

Unfortunately, several pupils were slightly hurt and the school had to be closed for the remainder of the day. The following day, the administrative and pupil-personnel-service staff held a series of discussions about the incident. Although some people thought that it was a solitary incident, apparently there had been other manifestations of intergroup conflicts in the past year. After much planning involving community members and family members as well as input from pupils and teachers, an ongoing group work program was established at the beginning of the next school year. Its focus was on bridging gaps and increasing sensitivity and understanding between white and African American students and preventing further incidents.

Children and adolescents belong to communities that are bounded by geography and culture. The community system influences the membership and character of the group. Group work with children and adolescents in community systems takes place in day treatment centers, juvenile homes, and residential settings (Welsh, 1984).

Adolescents in rural communities experience many of the same social problems, such as substance abuse and family problems, that their counterparts in urban communities encounter (Coward & Rose, 1982). Furthermore, as children proceed to adolescence their problems sometimes increase. In first and second grade, Judy occasionally refused to do what her teachers suggested. Her teachers talked to her parents about the difficulty, which was considered minor. Nonetheless, by third grade Judy had a high level of noncompliance with teacher requests. Furthermore, when Judy reached adolescence her obstinacy at home increased as well. She refused to do any chores at home. The crisis point occurred when Judy's grandmother fell in their home and Judy refused to help her up. Judy's parents sought private psychiatric care for her. After an evaluation Judy was labeled "oppositional." She was enrolled in a special education class in middle school and referred to a community group work program.

Educational Perspective

The setting, goals, method, and issues discussed in group work with children and adolescents in school and community systems often has an educational component. In school systems, the educational setting influences the method used and issues handled by the group. The importance of schooling to children and adolescents makes the educational perspective significant in community systems too. In a community-based group held for adolescents diagnosed with life-threatening diseases, the leaders invited health professionals, including public health nurses, to educate the members about the cause, treatment, and prognosis of the disorders.

Group work promotes the acquisition of knowledge, attitudes, and skills that constitute competent social and academic functioning in school and community systems. It is useful in enhancing traditional education, which is concerned with developing the competence of children and adolescents in such subjects as languages (see Chapter 9). Children and adolescents conduct much of their learning in groups, and group work can resolve problems that interfere with learning. Lester, a third-grade student with a speech impediment who joined a school-based academic achievement group, wondered if the group was a class. It appeared to be more informal and fun than a class and it dealt with learning. Lester learned to enjoy learning activities more and felt more rewarded by studying and working with other children in school. Lester told one of the leaders he thought the group was like a class. He told one of his friends that he wished his classes were more like the group.

Leaders intend that any changes that occur among members in the group will spread to encompass their functioning in school and community systems. For the purpose of improving school-related functioning, group work in the schools is most effective when provision is made for rapid and relatively direct application of learning gains to the rest of the school system. A high school group for Native American and Mexican American adolescents who were having academic difficulties focused on the development of study skills. The members learned to check their work, memorize information, and read rapidly. Furthermore, they helped each other study for tests. Each of the members had friends who were also having academic difficulties yet were not enrolled in such a group. In the latter sessions of the group, the members reported how they shared some of their skills with their friends. Several of those friends expressed an interest in joining such a group.

Social-emotional education represents a more recent, alternative, and complementary approach to traditional education. It aims at the attainment of competence in social-role functioning of children and adolescents and is closely related to group work. The Henry Hope school had provided a traditional education to the children of working-class and immigrant families for many years. When the school board appointed the new principal, the school system was in the midst of a great change in educational policy. The principal experimented with social-emotional education by hiring a teacher with expertise in developing and delivering an affective curriculum. The children in her class soon learned to identify and describe their own feelings and use their creativity in numerous artistic projects that they enjoyed.

The goals of education are important in assessing and promoting the processes and outcomes of group work. Two types of goals may be distinguished. Social goals, which are tied to socialization and social-emotional education, include improved human relations and group functioning. Marcus, a shy 16-year-old, was referred to a community group. Initially, Marcus sat speechless in a corner of the room where he fearfully peered out at the other members.

Although the leaders acknowledged Marcus's presence, they let him alone and concentrated on fostering an atmosphere of safety, respect, and good humor in the group. After a few sessions Marcus began to talk to one of the other members.

In contrast, academic goals, which are usually more often related to traditional education than social-emotional education, include the comprehension and development of cognitive skills in such subject matters as reading. Susan was referred to a school group owing to her failing grades in algebra and chemistry. As the only Amerasian girl in the group Susan felt isolated. Nonetheless, after a while the composition changed so that Susan had company.

Susan knew that she spent the same amount of time studying as other teenagers, so she was somewhat puzzled about why she was having difficulty. Nonetheless, after participating in an exercise in the group Susan became aware that she liked other subjects better. One of the leaders, a teacher, noticed Susan's love of languages.

Social and academic goals are interrelated; the achievement of one set of goals is likely to facilitate the achievement of the other. Furthermore, the overall development of children and adolescents is more likely to be successful if they attain both social and academic goals. Children and adolescents who are able to resolve social problems, improve social competence, and attain social goals are likely to be better able to attend to school problems, improve academic competence, and reach academic goals. Bernice had been angry ever since her mother died. She participated in a group work program, which focused on mourning and recovering from loss. Thereafter, she was better able to concentrate on her studies.

The effectiveness of group work in helping children and adolescents in academic and social domains increases its perceived value to staff members in school and community systems. At an academically oriented high school, several teachers privately scoffed at a group work program that was proposed at the beginning of the school year for children with difficulties in school performance. Nonetheless, at an informational meeting that was held at the end of the school year, the leaders provided evidence of an increase in attendance, a reduction in the proportion of dropouts, and an improvement in the grade point average of most members. Although one of the teachers continued to deride the program after the informational meeting, the other teachers vocally supported it. The following year, all teachers saw the value of the group work program and supported its operation in the school.

In school and community systems, group work that is educational in nature possesses a structured method of delivering content and often includes a curriculum. The issues discussed often pertain to education or the school system, including social relationships with peers, academic performance and the consequences of underperformance, and attendance and conduct in the schools. A community center offered several recreational programs for children and adolescents. A worker in one of the programs noted that many of the adolescents seemed to be having substantial difficulties at school. Consequently, the worker formed a community center group for adolescents, which focused on school.

Members from three different middle schools found it useful to share their experiences. Joshua, who thought he was in a difficult school, was particularly astonished at how demanding teachers at a neighboring school were in regard to homework assignments.

Organizational Perspective

The community system influences the receptivity to group work programs in schools. The values, mission, and functional effectiveness of school and community systems affect the inauguration and continuation of group work programs for children and adolescents. Schools and community agencies operate in an interorganizational environment that ultimately affects the availability and delivery of group work. The director of Harmony House, a community agency serving substance-abusing adolescents in a sparsely populated rural area, became concerned when Nantucket USA, a newly formed local affiliate of a national social service agency, began to offer group work that competed with the outreach group work that Harmony House offered.

Organizational auspices, staffing patterns, and interpersonal and interprofessional relationships of leaders markedly affect the value of group work for members. The impersonal organization of some school and community systems is sometimes experienced as emotionally unsupportive by children and adolescents. Miranda, a 16-year-old, was fearful about her outpatient appointments at a very large medical complex. Indeed, she got lost in the labyrinthine passageways and arrived very late for her first appointment. She subsequently joined a supportive community group for Hispanic adolescents.

The organizational dynamics of school and community agencies have an impact on the social and academic adjustment of children and adolescents (Freeman, 1985). School policies encompass school practices, such as rules for conduct and rule enforcement, which have an impact on problems manifested by youngsters. Written and unwritten rules set standards for attendance, academic performance, and acceptable activity and conduct in and out of classes. In school systems, group work is a part of the ongoing educational enterprise. On the basis of members' ages, social problems addressed, and proposed themes, leaders determine the optimal location of the group work program within the school curriculum. At a middle school, two group work programs were offered, including a preventive program about substance abuse in the health education class and a socialization program in the social studies class.

The compulsory, formal, and normative features of school systems are related to the availability and costs and benefits of the provision of group work. In most school systems, attendance and participation in education is required, the organizational structure is formal, and acceptable standards or agreements for social functioning have been established for the children or adolescents who are part of the system. In school systems, group work that attempts to redress social problems may be offered on a voluntary basis. Norms that are developed may be helpful to children and adolescents in school and community systems.

Elias, who was habitually late and disruptive, learned to attend promptly and speak in turn. Nonetheless, members also must learn to differentiate between group norms and norms of other systems.

Nadia, an immigrant from Russia, became accustomed to the American way of speaking frankly about conflicts she was experiencing. Nonetheless, Nadia realized that this would be considered inappropriate at the school she attended.

The size of the school or community agency influences patterns of communication about the activities of the group, alliances, and formality of group decision making (Fatout & Rose, 1995).

Although ethical and legal constraints curtail confidentiality, efforts are made to maintain the confidentiality of communications. Ariella, the leader of a health promotion group for preadolescents, received repeated phone calls from a mother about the well-being of her daughter. Although Ariella understood and empathized with the mother's concern, she felt very constrained about what she could actually disclose to her.

Leaders communicate to persons, including supervisors, outside of the group in regard to its effectiveness. Evaluation of success in attaining objectives involves a communication process, which includes asking family members, school personnel, and peers how members have changed and are functioning (see Chapter 4). Leaders converse with the parents of young members about how they may have benefited from participation. At one of the final meetings of a community friendship group for young children, parents were invited to hear leaders and members speak about the members' gains. Gary, a shy youngster, was so embarrassed about all the compliments he received that he cried.

Personnel Perspective

Group work in school systems is provided by a staff of diverse professional backgrounds who interact with teachers, administrators, and pupil-personnel-service providers. At a middle school, a nurse and a social worker collaborated to offer an educational group for adolescents to discuss public health concerns.

Power and social position influence the creation, organization, and development of innovative group work programs. Although the insider and the outsider possess power and use it effectively within school and community systems, it is likely to stem from different bases and to be applied differentially. The advantages of the insider social position include command of resources and professional relationships within the system and the ability to promote the continuity of the program. The insider is likely to have social power accrued from having developed working relationships within the agency. Janine had worked at a group home for almost 2 years and was well acquainted with all the children as well as many of the state staff. She was able to talk easily to her supervisor about starting a group.

In contrast, the outsider brings social position, prestige, power, and influence from an external organization to bear on the school or community system, provides resources, and establishes relationships within the system. Continuance of the program depends in part on the continued activity and success of the outsider in involving insider program staff. Latania worked for a federally supported housing and antipoverty program and impressed the members of the inner city school when she came to them with plans to develop a group work program to help pregnant adolescents.

Although highly experienced leaders may appear to have a favored social position in regard to establishing group work programs, novice professionals have the advantage of being permitted to try out novel ideas and make errors that will be more readily forgiven. Andrew, a new practitioner in the child and adolescent outpatient department of an urban community mental health center, knew that he had a lot to learn about group work programs. When he approached staff for referrals and only received the name of one child he pleaded ignorance to his supervisor and then developed a more effective recruitment strategy.

ATTITUDES TOWARD GROUP WORK

Perceptions among practitioners of the value of group work is used to secure the acceptance, support, and referral to programs. Furthermore, attitudes toward starting to develop group work programs for children and adolescents reflect the personality characteristics of key persons in the school or community agency and are a crucial ingredient in beginning and establishing a group work program (Hage & Aiken, 1980).

The principal of an inner-city middle school had a strong and powerful personality with high self-esteem. She led a school with high graduation rates in which the children did well on achievement tests and in which there were few discipline problems. After several parents came to talk to her about their children's unhappiness about some of the recent changes in the school, she referred them to her assistant principal and her pupil personnel staff. The guidance counselor developed and presented the principal with a plan to develop a structured group work program.

Related to experiences that people have had with or have heard about groups, attitudes toward group work with children and adolescents, which vary in acceptance and enthusiasm, affect the design, delivery, and support of group work. Attitudes toward group work are related to myths, concerns, and conceptions about the power, processes, and effects of groups. Angel, a recent immigrant from Puerto Rico, refused to have her youngest child, Salvador, participate in a community group because of her belief that he would acquire a mental disorder from the other children in the group.

Some individuals believe that groups have tremendous power and deviant values. In one public school, some of the parents refused to allow their preadolescent children to participate in groups because they were concerned that it would violate the religious teachings they were attempting to instill. The leader then met with the parents to allay their concerns. One of the parents preached from the Bible throughout the meeting.

Clarification and providing information are means of persuading and convincing skeptics of the value of group work. Leaders who wish to overcome indifference and opposition develop a proper rationale, with due and knowledgeable consideration of the advantages and limitations of using groups in school and community systems.

ADVANTAGES AND LIMITATIONS
OF GROUP WORK

Group work can be effective in addressing interpersonal and peer-related problems of children and adolescents. The efficiency advantage of concurrently serving multiple members who become increasingly well acquainted is particularly important in school and community systems where relatively few leaders are available. In school and community systems, children and adolescents have ready access to social situations that are important bases for the process of group work. Jacobi was frequently shaken down for money by peers in the middle school playground. When he became a member of a school group, Jacobi was able to discuss the situation and develop some ideas for handling it. In one role-play situation he developed a response that appeared to be effective in real life. Jacobi said, "If I had any money it would be in that store."

Some particular advantages of group work with children and adolescents are apparent in school systems (Berkovitz, 1987a, b). Members frequently are able to observe, become knowledgeable about, and support one another within the school system. A variety of personnel in the school system, including teachers, contribute to leaders' knowledge about the members. Furthermore, some specialized types of groups may be offered in the school system. Crisis intervention groups provide the benefit of offering immediate help in a setting where a crisis has occurred.

A 14-year-old boy hung himself in the living room of his separated parents' 15-room home. Many were stunned at the suicide of the son of a high-achieving family in this upper-class community. Although others had heard about teenagers committing suicide, it never had happened before in the school, in which Richard was one of the top students. A search was on for clues as to what had precipitated the suicide. Many were concerned that perhaps another child would make a suicide attempt. Within 24 hours of the event, mental health professionals commenced group work for children in the middle school Richard had attended to help youngsters grieve their loss, prevent additional suicide attempts, and restore equilibrium.

Agencies that have elaborate intake and registration procedures inadvertently block youngsters from receiving the group work that could be beneficial to them. Fortunately, some community agencies also provide group work, which is relatively accessible, often requiring a simple registration process and affordable fee.

Membership and attendance in the school system group tends to be relatively stable. Moreover, participation in groups in the normative environment of school systems reduces stigmatization, labeling, and financial barriers to access services (LeCroy & S. R. Rose, 1986). Indeed, many members greatly enjoy such groups.

Group work in school and community systems are complementary, such that the limitations of group work in schools (Berkovitz, 1987a, b) are actually the advantages of group work in community systems. In community systems, the actions of the members and the process of group work often tend to be less disruptive to the system. Privacy is more likely to be available, confidentiality is more likely to be kept, and rumors and gossip are often more contained in a community system group. In school system groups, ventilation of feelings about staff members is more likely to be revealed. Arleshia was a pupil who had strong feelings about all her teachers. Unfortunately, she disliked her ninth-grade biology teacher. When the other members discussed their teachers she couldn't keep this quiet in group. Despite the teenagers vowing to keep things that were discussed in the group, Mr. Mouch heard about it in the teachers' lounge. Although he never confronted Arleshia directly in his class, he had a difficult time teaching her in his class.

Consequently, some staff are more likely to undermine the group in the school system. Some teachers may feel that their own class is in competition with the group for the attendance, participation, and attention of the youngsters. Despite an agreement pledging support, Roger, a leader of a preventive health group for adolescents, discovered that Kristen, an eighth-grade teacher, refused to allow children from her class to attend sessions. One day Kristen told Roger that there was a special art project for the children to complete. Another time they had to review for special scholarship examinations. On yet another occasion a special guest came to class. Consequently, Roger met with Kristen and the assistant principal to resolve her objections.

Many limitations, such as the stressfulness of group work for some members, can be dealt with through effortful planning, composition, and organization (see Chapter 3). In preventive groups, leaders identify target children or adolescents who are at high risk for developing problems. Careful composition minimizes potential risks to children and adolescents. In a socialization group for fatherless boys held in a community center, the leader decided to include Bennie, who had been reported by juvenile authorities to be assaultive, on an experimental basis. The leader observed and supported Bennie, who though occasionally angry was not aggressive within the group.

Whereas many children and adolescents are able to participate in and benefit from group work, individual and family interventions also have value and can supplement group work. In an inner-city neighborhood, a parents' group was offered to complement a community group for children of alcoholics. Whereas many of the same themes were discussed in the parents' group, the material was presented from an adult viewpoint.

Furthermore, indirect practice modalities, such as community organization, also are useful ways of addressing the types of social problems that also are treated in group work. In a multiservice community center, group work was offered to contain adolescent violence. The program focused on identifying events that precipitated incidents of violence. The group worker consulted with a community worker who subsequently devised a community organization program to tackle poverty, unemployment, and underemployment, which were widespread.

CONCLUSION

From an ecological perspective, children and adolescents learn to function within interrelated social systems. Their experiences and conflicts reflect the social problems manifested in the schools in which they study and the communities in which they live.

Group work for children and adolescents are delivered within an organizational context. The availability and continuity of group work is influenced by the structure, functioning, and resources of school and community systems, and the power of those persons who initiate services. Attitudes toward group work with children and adolescents also have an effect on the support and development of such programs.

Education serves as a context for group work. In school systems, the position and characteristics of personnel who design and deliver group work have a notable impact on the development and adjustment of children and adolescents. In comparison to group work in school systems, group work in community systems largely has complementary advantages and limitations.

Chapter 2

THE BASIS OF GROUP WORK

In this chapter the theoretical underpinnings of group work with children and adolescents in school and community systems will be described. Children and adolescents are liable to experience many stressors, and how members think about and cope with stress is an important focus of group work.

STRESS THEORY

Life Transitions

An assumption of group work with children and adolescents is that many members lack the requisite skills and experience (Cowen, Hightower, Pedro-Carroll, & Work, 1989) to cope with stressful life transitions (Felner, Farber, & Primavera, 1983), some of which are normative. For instance, as members attempt to adjust to the transition of moving from a relatively contained, secure, and stable elementary school system to a more demanding middle-school system they are likely to experience stress from the new demands of the new school (Elias, Gara, & Ubriaco, 1985; Felner et al., 1983). Indeed, the transition from elementary school to middle school has been shown to have a harmful effect on youngsters who previously were free of any noticeable or significant difficulties (Elias et al., 1985; Pumfrey & Ward, 1976; Simmons, Blythe, Van Cleave, & Bush, 1979; Toepfer & Marani, 1980). Group work can be used to prevent such harmful effects. By providing opportunities for members to discuss stressful experiences, preventive group work helps members more quickly adjust to the new school. As part of the initial orientation and registration period at one middle school, groups were formed for all new students. Older students described their experiences, stress reduction activities and exercises were used, information was shared, and a supportive tone was adopted by the leaders.

In middle school, circumstances frequently arise that interfere with the expected academic and social performance of children (Elias et al., 1986). Such circumstances can be the subject of normative and preventive group work, especially in school systems. For example, in an urban middle school group work was used to discuss safety issues and methods for negotiating a hazardous neighborhood situation.

Some school transitions are related to major stressful life events, such as parental divorce. Indeed, the stressful impact of the breakup of their parents' marriage places many children at risk for major adjustment difficulties (Emery, 1988; Hetherington, Cox, & Cox, 1982; Wallerstein & Kelly, 1980). Group work for children of divorce is prevalent in many school systems, particularly in those urban communities where the parental divorce rate is high (see Chapter 6). Parental neglect, abuse, and death also are major stressors for many children (LeCroy & S. R. Rose, 1986). At a teaching hospital, a short-term group was formed for children who had recently lost a parent. Designed to prevent major emotional disturbances, the group helped children grieve for their parents. It provided emotional support for the children who felt abandoned, lost, and isolated.

Adolescents normatively experience stressors associated with physical development, social acceptance, and school performance. Along with her mother and younger brother, 12-year-old Marie had recently moved from a distant larger community where she had been an average student. Most of Marie's classmates in her new private school had been friends and acquaintances since kindergarten. For the first time in her life, Marie failed one course and received low grades in three additional courses. As Marie began having twitches her concerned mother took her for a checkup. The physician could find nothing physically wrong and referred Marie to a social worker, who encouraged her to participate in a newly formed group.

Adolescent members may experience stressors associated with pubertal changes, demands for and engagement in substance abuse and sexual activity, and fears and experience of early, unwanted pregnancy. In a regional community health center, three types of groups were formed for adolescents. In separate educational groups for girls and boys, presentations and discussions were held about physical, social, and emotional changes in adolescence. In a combined group for boys and girls, adolescents learned how to cope with peer pressure for undesirable, risky activities. A third group, which was held for pregnant adolescents, offered support, education, and linkages to social service resources.

Labeling

As peer relations assume greater importance to adolescent members so do the perceptions that they have of one another, which are often expressed in the form of labels. Group work that is designed to promote understanding and improve intergroup relations makes use of the labels that adolescents use in describing social groups. Adolescents who like sports, those who like studying, those who are members of minority cultures, and those who are substance abusers each apply labels to themselves and have labels applied to them. Indeed, group work has been used to promote self-esteem, self-pride, and identity development among poor black and Hispanic adolescents (Lopez, 1991; Parsons, 1988).

Adolescent members' socialization and perceptions of people with problems influence labeling. Adolescents who perceive others in positive terms are liable to label themselves positively. The type of labels, in regard to positive or negative valences, that adolescents receive and apply influences their identity and self-concept. In regard to intentions and consequences, members feel that positive labeling rewards people and enhances their social status, whereas negative labeling stigmatizes and stresses others and is often the operationalization of discrimination. Indeed, experience with group work with Latino, black, white, and Asian middle school children indicates that race often is an issue, prejudices may exist in groups, and stereotypes should be discussed (Bilides, 1990, 1992).

Adolescent members receive and apply labels in the context of their social relationships within and out of the group. Whereas most adolescent peer groups in high schools are positively labeled, one negatively labeled group tends to experience major academic, mental health, and substance abuse problems (Downs & Rose, 1991; Rose & Downs, 1989). Adolescent members are likely to belong to high school peer groups based on whether they are popular and controversial or whether they are rejected or neglected (Franzoi, Davis, & Vasquez-Suson, 1994). Adolescents who are rejected and neglected are likely to receive negative labels, to experience academic and social difficulties, and to form cliques that, as informal social peer groups, also are appropriate targets of group work.

To counter the deleterious effects of labeling, group work often aims to provide emotional sustenance through expressive activities to members who lack a constructive social network and adequate family system. Group work is useful for members who have experienced significant loss and grief, including the death of their parents. In practice, group work that is supportive may be combined with more instrumental or task-oriented approaches.

Disasters

Some children and adolescents may be exposed to disasters, namely, natural events, such as tornadoes, fires, floods, earthquakes, or hurricanes; technological events, such as accidents, airplane or vehicle crashes, or explosions; and human-made events, such as civil unrest, rioting, or violence, including bombings or shootings (Carll, 1994). Such traumatic events, which affect the life and well-being of youngsters and cause a stir in school and community systems, are the focus of group work. In a small midwestern community, most of the members of the high school ice hockey team were killed or injured in a plane crash. At the high school, group work was provided to the distraught classmates. Its comprehensiveness and supportiveness was useful in combating the trauma.

Some schools and communities have a large population that experiences crises and traumas, including violence, on a frequent basis. In one urban community center, an ongoing group work program was established for adolescents who were friends and relatives of victims of violence. The program began after a 15-year-old boy was accidentally killed in an incident in which a classmate had attempted to shoot a history teacher who had given the classmate a bad grade.

Leaders try to help members reduce the impact of an excessive amount of stress, which has the potential to produce significant undesirable health and mental health consequences. Timely preventive and early interventive group work can help reduce common reactions to disasters that include anxiety and posttraumatic stress disorder (Vogel & Vernberg, 1993), school difficulties and isolation (Yeast, 1994), and adjustment disorders, depressive states, panic disorders, pathological grief, phobic disorders, and reactive psychoses (Scott, 1994).

George had been a calm child until a tragedy that took the life of his older sister. Since then, he experienced a great deal of anxiety and was unable to concentrate on his school work or sleep at night. Nevertheless, his participation in group work, in which he shared such traumatic experiences with peers and learned how to relax, resulted in some improvement.

Responses of young school-age children alert adults to the possibility that the former have been exposed to traumatic stress (Eth & Pynoos, 1985; Johnson, 1989, 1992). Disorganization of cognitive functioning is seen in lowered attention span and perspective and increased confusion and immobility. Deverbalization involves showing distress rather than talking about it and includes acting out, anxious clinging, avoidances, and thematic play. Somatization entails the bodily manifestation of reactions to stress, including muscular aches and pains, change in appetite, and digestive and respiratory discomfort.

In group work with children who have experienced disaster, the members ordinarily sit together in a circle, which provides a sense of togetherness (Shelby, 1994). Members express their feelings, develop safety plans, recount the disasters they experienced, and overcome losses. The leaders subsequently correct misperceptions about the disaster, work with family members, and promote hope.

Adolescent members' reactions to stress, which may be perceived by adults, consist of withdrawal or acting out, depression or sadness, loss of control, inability to concentrate, irritability, disturbed sleep or eating patterns, intrusive thoughts and flashbacks, and emotional numbing (Carll, 1994). Adolescents who display extreme stress reactions are candidates for group work.

Indeed, both children and adolescents have to learn constructive means of identifying and coping with stressors in order to maintain their physical and mental health, school performance, and social development. Stress-management approaches to group work are likely to be applicable in schools with very high academic standards. In a private preparatory school an adolescent committed suicide in his senior year. Henry left a note indicating that by receiving a B in a chemistry course his chances of ultimately entering a medical school were ruined. Eventually, the school introduced a group work program aimed at establishing an appreciation among adolescents for their own work, a realistic view of their life chances, and the promotion of physical and social activities.

Although young children and adolescents experience stress and anxiety, due to their cognitive development, adolescents are more readily able to understand the abstract concepts of stress and anxiety. Consequently, group work with adolescents is more likely to use terminology of stress theory than group work with children, although both include the application and experiential aspects.

Crisis intervention is particularly useful in schools and communities where traumatic events have occurred. Critical incident stress debriefing is an effective form of group work with children and adolescents (Mitchell, 1983). After an assault on a high school student by a community resident took place, parents, community leaders, and students became very concerned about safety. Group work was used to help the adolescents work through the incident and return to their prior adaptive level of functioning.

THOUGHT PROCESSES

Social Cognition

A fundamental assumption underlying group work with children and adolescents is that members think, process information, make decisions, solve problems, and interact within social contexts and situations. Furthermore, how members of various ages think about social situations tends to vary developmentally. Childhood social cognition tends to be concrete, undifferentiated, and focuses on observable stimulus features (Chandler, 1976; Shantz, 1983). Consequently, group work with young children focuses on concrete discussions and events. Stimulus materials, including posters, stories, and music, which are of interest to members of this age, are prepared by the leaders. By the ages of five to seven, children understand that others' thoughts may differ from their own thoughts, and they have a basic understanding of intention and consequences (Shantz, 1975). Therefore, leaders explicitly ask young child members how they think about and understand social situations that are described in the sessions.

In order to ensure a consistent basis for understanding of events by members, leaders repeatedly enact, describe, and discuss social situations.

Members in middle childhood readily think about uncomplicated social situations from the perspective of other persons and recognize that others have an inner experience. Members realize that others also are thinking about them, including their thoughts, feelings, and intentions. Discussions proceed on the basis of their understanding of people and of human nature, including their concerns and anxieties about what people think of them.

As children move into adolescence their social cognition becomes more abstract, differentiated, and focuses on unobservable psychological features (Livesley & Bromley, 1973). Adolescent members are able to observe themselves and interpersonal situations more objectively and comprehensively and are often better able to explain and describe interpersonal situations than younger children. Group work with adolescents includes occasional forays into philosophical discussions and attempts to align objective and critical views of the self with subjective and supportive views. Alexandra, a 13-year-old in a community group, voiced many negative characteristics about her personality and her appearance. The leader countered this by asking the members for their opinions, which inevitably balanced Alexandra's disapproving views.

As youngsters develop from childhood through adolescence they pass through stages in which complex mixes of dependence, independence, and interdependence are present. Leaders must be prepared for such different mixes. In a third-grade boys group, the leaders were surprised to find that David, a seemingly independent young boy, began to act in a dependent fashion with the leaders and the members. On inquiry they discovered that he was experiencing considerable stress in the family setting.

Developmental factors influence members' responses to disruption in their parents' marriage, perceptions of family changes, and coping patterns (Cowen et al., 1989). Feelings of sadness, confusion, guilt, and fear of abandonment have been identified as key emotional reactions among 6- to 8-year-olds (Wallerstein & Kelly, 1980). With such children, the leaders are in the position of improving mood, dispelling confusion and guilt, and rationally examining fear of abandonment. Loyalty conflicts, anger, and issues of stigma and isolation have been identified as the major concerns for 9- to 12-year-olds (Wallerstein & Kelly, 1980). With such children, conflict resolution strategies can be used to reduce being pulled between the parents. Also, constructive means of working through anger should be addressed.

Problem Solving

The origins of problem-solving approaches may be traced to such philosophers as John Dewey (1933), whose phases of reflective thinking are akin to the phases of group problem solving. For instance, intellectual formulation of a question is related to conceptualizing a problem. The use of suggestions to form a hypothesis is akin to gathering ideas from members and leaders to understand the problem. Reasoning in reflective thinking involves thinking things through or means-ends problem solving. Hypothesis testing involves trying out a particular solution.

Preparation by the leaders, collaboration between the leaders and the members, and cooperation between the members promote problem solving (Somers, 1976). Leaders promote effective and productive problem solving among members and maintain a balance between individual and group concerns. In a group for young children, the members persisted in talking about their own interests, hobbies, and activities. The leader used an activity that required them to work as a unit in pretending they were members of an airline crew.

Leaders serve as guides for the problem-solving process and help members evaluate the success of the group, which is based on the participation of the members, who become aware of themselves as participants in the process. At the conclusion of a yearlong middle school group, the leaders discussed how each member contributed to the group.

Problem-solving approaches are useful in working with members who have the capacity for comprehending questions or issues that are stressful to the members involved and that call for resolution through decision making and discussion methods. It is assumed that most members are more effective problem solvers in some domains and can benefit from targeted help in their less effective domains to improve their problem-solving abilities.

George, a member of a middle school group, was excellent in solving school problems but felt lost in making friends. When a friend would call to suggest an activity for the same day, if George was busy he would simply say he was unable to go and would abruptly hang up. Whereas preventive group work is designed to enhance the functioning of children and adolescents without identified problems, interventive group work is intended to help youngsters with identified problems. Nora Blixen, a public health social worker, formed a preventive group for 9- and 10-year-olds that was designed to forestall substance-abuse-related difficulties encountered by many adolescents in the tricounty region that she served.

In structured, time-limited groups, problem-solving approaches have the advantage of being specific, prescriptive, concrete, and replicable. Problem-solving approaches are often understandable, applicable, and widely accepted in school and community systems. They are useful in dealing with immediate problems and as a way of thinking that will increase the probability members will be able to successfully handle future, related problems. As an adolescent, Toni was a member of a group that helped her deal with dating situations, which made her uncomfortable. She kept in touch with the leader. As a young woman, Toni reported that the skills she acquired in the group were useful in her marriage.

Problem solving is an important component of group work with children and adolescents, which includes promoting social cognition, stress reduction, supportive peer relations, and reducing labeling. Problem-solving approaches are characterized by a systematic attempt to develop and train the cognitive skills of children and adolescents. When action or activity problems of members are present, a performance component, such as role playing, complements the cognitive orientation of problem solving. Leaders ensure that the skills that are to be acquired are relevant for adaptation in particular settings. Leaders consider the cultural context in using direct training to promote the acquisition of problem-solving skills (Cowen et al., 1989).

Group work to develop the social competency of children and adolescents considers such factors as variations in cultural norms in regard to eye contact, physical proximity, and interpretations of assertiveness (see Chapter 7). Henry had considerable difficulties with peers in his sixth-grade class who mistook his respectful averting his glance for disinterest and inattention.

Problem-solving approaches help members acquire and strengthen their interpersonal skills. Group work designed to promote interpersonal-cognitive problem-solving skills acquisition provides a cognitive map, or schematic, for helping members identify and resolve personal and interpersonal difficulties.

Personal experiences of social problems include conflicts experienced by members. Interpersonal-cognitive problem solving (Spivack, Platt, & Shure, 1976) or social problem solving (Elias et al., 1986) involves a sensitivity and willingness to recognize and acknowledge the existence of a problem. Louise's social worker thought she might benefit from being in a group, as she noticed that Louise tended to deny having any problems.

Furthermore, problem solving includes the members being cognizant and able to verbalize and set goals. Young members often have an intuitive sense of difficulties that may occur between people. Adolescent members are likely to conceptualize and verbalize their feelings, set goals, and be aware of the potential for difficulties that occur between people as a result of conflict and aggression.

The imaginative and speculative faculties of the mind are useful in problem solving with young members. Leaders ask young members to originate and respond to creative descriptions of problem-solving situations. In group work with 6- and 7-year-olds, Marcy and Sue asked the members to consider how dragons could get along better with one another. Members develop their ability to think of alternative ways of coping with or solving problems and attaining goals in situations. For each of the alternatives, members think of the potential interpersonal consequences of problem-solving actions.

Problem solving encompasses decision making in selecting potential solutions. From an array of possibilities that are generated, members select one that appears workable. The alternative that is selected comes into play after an action has been implemented.

Leaders encourage members to avoid becoming preoccupied with thinking about a goal to the exclusion of thinking about the means that would be useful for reaching that goal (Spivack & Shure, 1974). Richard, a 15-year-old member of a community group, perseverated in discussing how much money he would like to make yet was reluctant to consider the possibility of taking a part-time job after school. Members plan particular ideas for implementing a potential solution, consider possible obstacles to implementation, and carry out attempts to reach particular solutions. Adolescent members who have well-developed means-ends problem-solving abilities recognize that a sequence of interrelated events may be necessary to eventually reach a desired goal.

The initiative of members is helpful in yielding constructive problem resolution (Bandura, 1977). The leaders encourage the members' belief that they can overcome emerging obstacles and set the expectation that it is sometimes necessary to try another solution, as even well-planned solutions only work some of the time.

Members in or past middle childhood have the potential to understand that their own feelings and actions are closely related to, and influence and are influenced by, the feelings and actions of others. The capacity to think about how others think and feel and to recognize complications in interpersonal situations is seen in the members' interactions and their discussions of material from their own lives.

After implementing a potential solution, members evaluate its success in reaching an interpersonal goal and resolving a problem. Nevertheless, if the problem still exists or an additional one has emerged, the members return to an earlier stage of the process and proceed to try out yet another solution.

The process is complete when the problem is ultimately resolved.

GROUP WORK DEVELOPMENTS

Early forms of group work tended to be relatively unstructured nondirective approaches, such as activity therapy (Schiffer, 1983; Slavson & Schiffer, 1975). More recent forms tend to have a greater degree of structure, as expressed in the organization of assessment, prevention, intervention, and evaluation procedures. Such directive approaches tend to be highly prescriptive in regard to leadership and presume that leaders initiate clear plans of action. Directive approaches, which use assignments for members, appear to be useful with many younger children and, in a modified way, with adolescents too.

Socialization through activity is a major function of group work with children and adolescents. Norms for intragroup activity usually emphasize skills training. Socialization and social skills training groups, which provide services that once were more regularly provided by families, aim to improve social competence. Increasingly, structured school and community groups tend to be organized on a thematic basis. Psychoeducational and focus groups focus on such topics as AIDS prevention, parental divorce, substance abuse, suicide prevention, anger control, and relaxation (Jaffe & Kalman, 1991). Some thematic groups allow members to come and go freely and are open-ended throughout their sessions. Nevertheless, to promote cohesion among members and allow for personal matters to be discussed in depth, many groups are open to new membership only in beginning or in subsequent reformulation phases.

Short-term or time-limited groups, including many closed-ended thematic groups, are the most prevalent and, in certain aspects, the most appropriate, time-efficient type of group work. Whereas many children and adolescents make sufficient progress in short-term groups, others could benefit from a longer-term group.

Marguerite was a shy girl who had few friends. In group work, she began to develop new social skills. Nevertheless, the group met for only one month. Her mother talked to the leader, who agreed that Marguerite could benefit from more group work. Furthermore, whereas short-term groups are suitable for skill development, personality and character changes are more suitably the focus of long-term groups, which ideally would be offered to youngsters to a greater degree than is currently the case. Alex was a high school junior whose reluctance to interact with his peers and adults was becoming more pronounced. A member of the pupil-personnel-services team referred Alex to an innovative yearlong group psychotherapy program, which was able to provide him with some noticeable benefits.

Members participate in many natural and formed groups, which are major vehicles for socialization as well as sites for spontaneously occurring social play. Peer groups have the potential to offer members social support, which is directly related to adjustment (Kurdek, 1987). In school systems, peer-led tutoring groups involve sharing of instructional capacities and providing opportunities for older children to help younger ones and, in doing so, themselves. Nevertheless, some members, who could benefit from such added support avoid participation in peer groups because they feel different and isolated (Cowen et al., 1989).

In some instances, group work with children and adolescents, which ordinarily is led by one or two adults, develops into a peer-led group. The first sessions of an activity group for early adolescents, which were held at an after-school recreation center, were organized and conducted by an adult volunteer.

Afterward, most of the major leadership functions were assumed by the members. The adult remained available at the center and provided some guidance, supervision, and set limits for the members. On one occasion the members wanted to take the community center van and drive to a nearby state for a party. The adult vetoed their idea and helped them develop a more feasible alternative.

CONCLUSION

Many children and adolescents who experience difficulties in family and peer relationships, health and mental health, and school performance may be helped through group work. Underlying group work is the recognition of the influence of cognitive development of members, the use of problem solving, the role of stress, and the nature of labeling processes. A directive, structured, and time-limited mode of group work is often an efficient way of helping members. Leaders help members pass through developmental transitions and acquire thinking and performance skills in their interpersonal relationships. The following chapter describes principles of planning, composition, and assessment.

Chapter 3

PROCESSES OF PRACTICE

Group work with children and adolescents in school and community systems constitutes a series of interrelated actions by leaders. The present chapter presents the sequence of actions that precede the sessions, namely planning, composition, and assessment, and describes the preventive-interventive actions and techniques that are useful during their beginning, middle, and ending phases.

PLANNING

The lives of children and adolescents tend to be structured around the school year, and many problems that youngsters have show up at school. Julie was a bright youngster, whose teachers noticed that she spent an inordinate amount of time staring into empty space. Her parents considered the difficulty serious when it was brought to their attention by the school.

The scheduling of community groups is in line with that of school groups although the former are also held during the summer. Owing in part to the time involved in organizing a new group, school and community groups usually begin meeting sometime after the start of the school year.

Nonetheless, group work may begin earlier when a group is planned in advance, is part of an ongoing program of service delivery, or when processes of referral begin earlier. In the first year of its operation, a group work program for sexually abused children had started its sessions in November. Nonetheless, in its second year its sessions began in October and the group therefore was able to meet for a longer period.

The potential desirable effects of planning include positively influencing the motivation of the members, increasing the ability of leaders to predict the process, and increasing the likelihood of success in meeting objectives. Prior to convening the group, leaders should seek permission, approval, and support from family, school, and community systems. Parents and guardians who encourage member attendance and participation and who cooperate and collaborate with leaders promote the success of the group and the members' well-being. Leaders prepare and distribute permission slips and release-of-information forms to gather material for assessment (McWhinney, Haskins-Herkenham, & Hare, 1991).

Initially, leaders consider the purposes of the group. Preventive purposes are for members to maintain their sound functioning and resilience to stress, improve their ability to solve problems in the future, and forestall the development of new problems. Interventive purposes are to enhance current functioning, improve coping skills to reduce stress, and resolve current problems.

The leaders then design the temporal structure of the group in accordance with the members' ages and the type of system. In school systems, sessions are often one class period in length. For young children, brief 30-minute sessions are helpful in maintaining attention whereas adolescents are often comfortable with longer, 45-minute sessions.

To promote continuity between sessions, young children usually require shorter intervals between sessions than adolescents. Whereas groups for young children may require two sessions per week, groups for adolescents may work well meeting once a week.

In school systems, the meeting place is planned in relationship to the classes and curriculum. A group work program for adolescent children of disabled parents was proposed in a large high school. It was to be offered during a recess period immediately following a health education class. In the contracting process, leaders elicit member cooperation in arriving at an agreement regarding the responsibilities of the parties, activities, and evaluation. In the early phase of a community group for pregnant adolescents, all aspects of the group were considered. Then, the leaders drew up a written agreement that indicated that all parties agreed to regularly attend sessions, respect and assist one another, participate in lectures, discussions, and role plays, watch educational videotapes, and complete final evaluation forms.

Recruitment of members includes a consideration of group size, ages and characteristics of members and, in school groups, grade levels and classrooms. Anticipating some attrition for a community group of about eight fatherless boys, the leaders decided to recruit 10 boys. Although the original plan called for all members to be 13 years of age the leaders decided to recruit 12- to 14-year-old members.

The organization of the entire series of sessions are planned prior to convening the group. Agendas, including a description of materials, activities, and the amount of time to be devoted to each activity, are written for each session. Of course, some events are unplanned, and some degree of flexibility is required in following the plan. The fourth session of a socialization group for isolated rural children was to be devoted to sports. Nonetheless, Hiram lost his sister Mary in a farm machinery accident 2 days earlier, and the group mourned the tragedy with Hiram and his family.

To gather information and maintain communication with and support from the external environment, leaders collaborate with persons in a variety of systems. Planning the collaborations includes establishing a list of persons in school, community, and family systems with whom to meet. At times, it is more feasible to collaborate with the parents of young children than it is to collaborate with the parents of adolescents. The leaders of an adolescent health education group were surprised at the reluctance of members and parents to engage one another in a joint meeting held at the end of the group.

Leaders consider the desired ends of public relations, such as notification about the existence of particular groups and the creation of additional groups, and the means of communication, such as the use of a newsletter, telephone calls, and school-home notes. Sharing evaluation findings also is planned. Nonetheless, constraints exist as to informing those in family, school, and community systems of progress (McWhinney et al., 1991).

Confidentiality should be maintained so that little personal information divulged by the members is disclosed. Nonetheless, group-level information readily may be shared with parents. The leaders of a community group for children sent monthly statements to the parents about the topics that were discussed in the group.

In school systems, it is often beneficial for leaders to invite teachers to join the classroom discussion for one or more sessions as it demystifies the activities, fosters a bridge to the members' education, and promotes a better understanding on the part of the teachers (Kovnat, 1979).

COMPOSITION

Composition, which influences process and outcome, takes place within the constraints of size. For appropriate quality and quantity of interaction to occur, a minimum of four members and a maximum of about 12 members is required. A smaller group usually requires regular attendance and active participation whereas a larger one requires maintaining task and goal-centered direction.

Prior to actually convening the group, leaders develop an explicit set of guidelines for composition. Two types of criteria are developed by leaders. Inclusion criteria, which encompass the capacities of potential members to function constructively, consist of desirable characteristics of members that will favorably influence interaction. A social worker in a community mental health center was interested in forming a group for adolescents. The inclusion criteria she considered were the ability to be verbal and the ability to participate in role playing.

Exclusion criteria refer to characteristics of children or adolescents that will result in their being assessed as ineligible or unsuitable for participation. Youngsters who are deemed unsuitable for one group often are considered to be suitable for participation in another type. George was referred for group work; however, the leaders wanted an even balance between girls and boys in the group and therefore decided to refer him to a group that had an opening for a boy.

Leaders consider a range of potential similarities and differences among the children or adolescents who will make up the group. To provide a common base of support to the members, a measure of homogeneity, in which members have shared or common characteristics, is desired. To promote rational decision-making and problem-solving processes, some degree of heterogeneity also is desirable. Indeed, a balance between homogeneity and heterogeneity is usually best. As member characteristics, cultural factors are sometimes a source of homogeneity. As a source of heterogeneity, however, a diversity of cultural factors in composition provides members with an opportunity to relate to peers of dissimilar backgrounds.

To maintain children in the group, it is essential that at least two representations of a race are present (Bilides, 1990). Furthermore, racially mixed groups (such as, of Latino, black, white, and Asian children) tend to be composed of subgroups that reflect majority or minority power issues in school systems (Bilides, 1992). Mary grew up in a small midwestern town with persons whose religious background and beliefs were similar to her own. In a 2-week statewide summer residential group work program for adolescents, which focused on academic skills, she lived with youngsters from diverse ethnic backgrounds. To Mary's surprise she found out, as she put it, that they were "fellow human beings." To attain balanced composition, a practice principle is to have at least one sociodemographic or descriptive characteristic in common to provide a basis for cohesion and some variation in the performance or behavioral characteristics of members to promote lively interaction (Bertcher & Maple, 1985; Goldstein, Heller, & Sechrest, 1966). The leaders of an insight group for adolescents at a community mental health center included several members who were shy and several who were outgoing.

Some groups that consist entirely of leaders and members of the same sex allow the former to model identity development. Furthermore, some sensitive concerns are more easily handled with greater privacy, support, and understanding within same-sex groups.

In contrast to same-sex groups, mixed-sex composition provides a wider range of opportunities for modeling, role playing, and feedback. To reduce the chance of isolation and scapegoatism, a mixed-sex group should be evenly balanced in regard to the number of girls and boys. Indeed, the composition guideline of having at least two members of each sex in the group often is insufficient for proper social-emotional functioning of the group. A school achievement group for inner-city third-grade children consisted of eight boys and four girls. All the boys formed friendships within the group. Furthermore, two of the girls (one African American and one white) became close friends. Unfortunately, the other two girls (one African American and one white) feared and disliked one another. At the urging of the parents, the leaders attempted to promote friendship between the latter two girls. The parents' discussions with the principal centered on finding additional girls for the group. Two weeks later one more girl joined the group.

The age and gender of the members tend to influence interaction. In middle childhood a sociometric divide tends to exist between girls and boys such that same-sex groups are often more cohesive than mixed-sex groups. In adolescence, the sociometric distance between girls and boys has lessened. Nonetheless, attraction between heterosexual members, which can enliven the dynamics, also can serve as a distraction and a potential obstacle to goal attainment. In a recreational group for 15-year-old boys and girls, Jose interrupted Maria whenever she spoke. Usually, Maria blushed, was flustered, and was unable to continue speaking. Ultimately, the leaders adopted a strict rule about interruptions for all the members.

Closeness of age, with accompanying similarity in physical, cognitive, and social-emotional developmental levels, is directly related to shared interests and concerns. In school systems, groups usually are composed of youngsters who are similar in age and grade level. Although the usual age-grade correspondence is such that youngsters in the same grade usually are good candidates for being in the same group, some groups are composed of children with a greater age difference. For instance, cross-age tutoring groups, which are often composed of members of two different grades, involve the older children helping the younger ones with school subjects.

ASSESSMENT

Leaders are able to implement broad-based assessments of the social systems of members. For instance, through conducting an assessment, leaders are able to learn about the family background and current living circumstances of the members.

The assessment of individual members is an essential aspect of group work. Initial assessments determine youngsters' eligibility for program participation. For instance, psychoeducational assessments determine the eligibility of youngsters for enrollment in special education programs. If the initial assessments result in the youngsters being admitted to the program, subsequent assessments determine whether they will be admitted to the group. At times, the two types of assessment, which are usually carried out consecutively, occur simultaneously. For instance, Jack was assessed and found to be eligible to participate in a community program and in one of its groups. He enrolled as a member of a local "Y" and became a member of one of their physical and health education groups.

Mental Health

An awareness by the leaders of the mental health difficulties of members is significant for recruitment, composition, and process. The DSM (Diagnostic and Statistical Manual of Mental Disorders) is widely used as a categorization system for the mental disorders of individual members (American Psychiatric Association, 1994). Although diagnosis of mental disorders is necessary for the provision of group work in community mental health services, it is usually optional in school systems.

Attention deficit and disruptive behavior disorders are likely to be represented in populations that are served by group work in school and community systems. Furthermore, some members of mental health groups have multiple mental disorders. In a community mental health group for substance-abusing adolescents, one of the five members also received individual services outside of the group for depression.

Measures

Some measures that are used by leaders are broadly applicable. For most groups, the Adolescent Coping Orientation for Problem Experiences is a useful measure of the ways in which adolescents cope with difficulties and stress (McCubbin & Thompson, 1991). The Persistence Scale for Children, which measures perseverance in children ages 7 to 13

(Lufi & Cohen, 1987), also is useful for a wide range of groups, including those focused on academic achievement, as it measures determination to overcome obstacles.

As a measure of how adolescents describe their nonassertive, assertive, and aggressive responses in social situations, the Assertiveness Scale for Adolescents is particularly useful in social competence groups (Lee, Hallberg, Slemon, & Haase, 1985). Deluty (1979) has developed a valuable measure for measuring the assertiveness of children.

The Child's Attitude Toward Father and Mother Scales, which indicate how much stress is experienced and what the potential for violence is in adolescents' relationships to their parents, are particularly useful in group work centering on family concerns (Hudson, 1992). The Children's Beliefs About Parental Divorce Scale, which measures the views of children and adolescents of the parental situation, is helpful in group work with children of divorce (Kurdek & Berg, 1987).

The Depression Self-Rating Scale, which taps the level of depression in children between ages 7 and 13, is useful in group work dealing with mental health issues (Birelson, 1981). A similar measure, the Hopelessness Scale for Children, has been developed by Kazdin, French, Unis, Esveldt-Dawson, and Sherick (1983).

Such measures are administered to individuals in classes and in groups. By participating in schools, most children and adolescents are accustomed to filling out forms and reports and taking exams. Therefore, they already possess a cognitive set pertaining to completing measures. Usually, for children, assessments that have an element of fun are easily implemented. Nonetheless, there are limitations to which young children will be involved in assessment periods that are lengthy or that demand advanced reading and writing skills.

Whereas many measures are designed to be completed by the youngsters themselves, some measures are based on the perspectives of persons who observe the youngsters, such as their parents. The Homework Problem Checklist, an instrument that measures the homework problems of elementary school children between ages 6 and 10, is particularly useful for group work dealing with achievement difficulties (Anesko, Scholock, Ramirez, & Levine, 1987).

ACTIVITIES, PROCESSES,
AND TECHNIQUES

To maximize the knowledge, information, and support available to all participants, many children's groups are co-led. Coleadership involves the melding of styles, the development of a working relationship, the sharing of tasks in the preparation and conduct of the group, and teamwork. A useful pattern includes cooperation between an established professional leader and a novice professional leader. Interpersonal difficulties and personality conflicts related to diverse leadership styles should be recognized, managed, and resolved. A school achievement group for fifth-grade children was co-led. Lucy was married, affluent, and the mother of five children. Many parents of the children in her group had expressly requested that she be their child's leader. Mary was recently married, middle class, and childless. She had much international experience and had spent her summers teaching English in China. In regard to leadership styles, Lucy was flexible, used much humor, and had her favorites, whereas Mary was systematic, serious, and accepting of all youngsters.

Ultimately, the two leaders found they were unable to overcome their personal and professional differences and formed two different groups. Lucy's group was composed mostly of children whose backgrounds were similar to her own, and Mary's group was composed of children from diverse backgrounds.

To fulfill the purposes of the group within school and community systems, leaders implement a program of planned and organized session activities that vary on the six dimensions of prescriptiveness, controls, movement, competence, interactiveness, and rewards (Vinter, 1985). The *prescriptiveness* of the pattern of constituent performances refers to the extent to which rules guide the activity. In a community recreational group, members regularly played board games according to definite rules. *Institutionalized controls* govern participant activity. Persons act in a role to enforce the rules of the activity. The members participated in sports that were overseen by one child who took the role of umpire. *Provision for movement* refers to the extent to which the activity is physical. Playing sports involved more movement and complemented playing board games. *Competence* required for performance refers to the minimum ability required to engage in the activity. A new child who knew how to skip rope and play many other games joined the group. *Provision for participant interactiveness* is the extent to which verbal and nonverbal engagement is induced by the activity. One member went off to look at a book of pictures of the group but was asked by a leader to join the other children in playing on the swings.

Reward structure encompasses the types, amounts, and distribution patterns available to participants. At the end of the group a ceremony was held. Each member's name was called out and each received several badges for participation in the group activities.

The impact of activities is based on which members participate as well as the demands and limitations imposed by the structure of the activity (Gump & Sutton-Smith, 1955). Recreational activities, which have boundaries of time and place, tend to promote socialization. Games are usually acceptable and satisfying to members. The leaders of a community group developed a board game to help young members develop skills in saving and spending their allowances.

The availability and consumption of food, including snacks, increases the attractiveness of the group to most children and adolescents. Some groups are held over a lunch hour, and youngsters bring their own food to eat. Others include the preparation of food as an activity. Different types of food are appropriate for different ages and cultures. In a social values group conducted at a religious institution, the adolescent members enjoyed preparing potato pancakes.

Developmental Aspects

Leaders select arts and crafts to conform to the developmental level of the members. Creative activities and materials are particularly useful with children. Members who make drawings express feelings that are difficult to express verbally. Puppet shows dramatize social situations to elementary-school-age children and along with pictorial illustrations and cartoons (Hugill, Hindmarch, Woolford, & Austen, 1987) provide an impetus for conversation (Lokken, 1982). Children prepare illustrations and cartoon strips and then enact them in role-play situations (Hugill et al., 1987). Storytelling is useful as a way of illustrating problem-solving concepts and making them real, concrete, and understandable to children. Movements within children's groups include rolling, sliding, swinging, and bouncing. The following movement activities usually take place in pairs (Sherborne, 1990): In "rocks" one youngster pretends to be a rock and the other attempts to push the rock over. In "knees" one youngster pretends to wind, pull, or sew up the other and then drops, pushes, or cuts the thread so the other's knees fall down. "Sculptures" involves having one member move the other's arms and legs to form a sculpture.

Many creative and artistic activities are useful for a wide age range of children and adolescents, although they are modified for particular ages. A group photograph journal has been used with children involved in sexual abuse (Ross & Bilson, 1981). Through seeing themselves as others view them, photography and video are useful for increasing children's self-awareness (Walsh, Richardson, & Cardey, 1991). Such techniques provide feedback to adolescents about their appearance and self-concept (Furman, 1990; Hogan, Schaffer, & Villanueva, 1982). Skits and social dramas are planned, created, produced, and videotaped for closed-circuit television (Darrow & Lynch, 1983; Shinar, 1983).

Relaxation

Children and adolescents can benefit from stress inoculation training. Relaxation training methods are useful ways of reducing stress (Kochendofer & Culp, 1979). Relaxation techniques are useful in calming anxiety-ridden children so that they are able to attend to stories (Guggenbuhl, 1991). Indeed, various methods of relaxation are useful with children, including alternately tensing and relaxing muscle groups (Randolph, 1982) and thinking of relaxing places and situations. The children become aware of their physical reactions to stress and describe their bodily reactions, such as having the jitters. Then, they describe some of the stressors or events that lead them to feeling anxious or nervous. Afterward, they further describe physical reactions to stress and, finally, they report relaxing events and situations.

Relaxation promotes acceptance and encouragement of communication among members (Roe, 1993). Members are permitted to be expressive and sound is expected within sessions. To maintain the interest and enjoyment of members, activities are varied and of brief duration. By design, some activities, such as role playing, are repeated with variations in regard to roles, content, and focus.

The frequency of use of activities is based on their value to the leaders as well as the members' expressed interests.

In order for group work to provide a basis for members to function better in their social environment, a cooperative atmosphere that permits sound communication is established. The group provides opportunities for choice in friendship, development of peer relationships, and provision of support. Modeling and feedback processes, with the optional use of videotaping, are directed by leaders toward attaining the purposes of the group. Leaders use structuring techniques to form smaller groups within the larger one.

Alliances form based on friendship and similarity of sociodemographic characteristics. To foster supportive social relationships, leaders establish a buddy system, a paired peer-helping relationship that provides a structured opportunity for dyadic helping processes to take place. Buddies are usually of the same sex and age and, in school systems, share one or more classes. The buddy provides feedback about and concretizes areas of difficulty or problems that the other member experiences (Fujii, 1989). Stephanie's buddy Sarah was confused about boys who wanted an exclusive dating relationship with her. In a phone conversation the day after a group session, Stephanie told Sarah that her difficulty was related to being too involved with too many boyfriends. Although Sarah saw her situation in different terms she appreciated Stephanie's attentive listening and support.

Discussion

The group is a forum for identifying self-defeating thoughts and attitudes, generating new and self-affirming thoughts, making decisions, and solving problems. The development of cognitive skills that can be used outside of the sessions increases the members' conviction that they truly have gained something valuable.

Formal and structured discussion is used as a problem-solving method. Discussion also is used as a means of explaining techniques and activities to members. Through participation in discussions some members' self-esteem may be temporarily elevated (Kovnat, 1979).

Thematic groups tend to rely on discussion of topics of concern to members. In a community center group, the adolescent members generated and prioritized a list of subjects that they wanted to discuss. The subjects selected were dating, violence, and school, respectively. Two sessions were devoted to each topic.

Audiovisual materials often are valuable adjunctive tools for thematic or educational discussions. In a health promotion group for children, the leaders showed videotapes of proper dental care, good nutrition, and sports.

Several discussion techniques are useful in group work. As an opener or ice breaker, rounds, also known as the technique of bad news, good news, allow for the consideration of problematic topics, which end on an optimistic note. The technique of rounds allows each member in sequence to either comment on a topic or pass and has been used for evaluation (Womersley, 1993).

A circular seating arrangement promotes full verbal and nonverbal communication and visibility between members. It lends itself to standing, to movement, and provides a sense of drama if the circle is closed and the members enact a role-play sequence within it. The use of tables and chairs is beneficial to moderate the intensity of the circular arrangement, to reduce the vulnerability that members sometimes experience, and for some activities involving arts and crafts or writing. The Magic Circle, which involves all members and transfers leadership to them, consists of using active listening skills, focusing on feelings, paraphrasing statements, reviewing prior material, and pointing out similarities and differences (Fisher, 1989).

The brainstorming technique, which can be presented to members as a game, serves as a disinhibitor and confidence builder and is used to develop many creative and novel thoughts. Within a brief predetermined time period of several minutes, members develop as many ideas as possible, refrain from criticisms, and add on to and come up with any and all ideas, including the most outrageous. Brainstorming can be used in the entire group or in subgroups.

Role Playing

Role playing is an imaginative and enjoyable activity that is well suited for use with children and adolescents. In role playing, members simulate a real-life social situation and are able to benefit through increased understanding of self and others.

Whereas some role plays require only a couple of active members, others involve the participation of all members. Leaders assign a maximum number of members to roles. Some roles require active participation whereas others emphasize observation.

Initially, leaders prepare situations that illustrate hypothetical, commonly experienced difficulties. In a community group for late adolescents who wished to develop friendships with members of the opposite sex, the leaders presented a role-play situation in which one person asked the other to a dance. Later, members prepare situations that illustrate actual difficulties that they have experienced.

Initially, the leaders determine what the role-play situation is and who will get to play which part (Lovins & Bogal, 1980).

Members receive instruction on the roles that they have to play.

To convey realism, the social situation, which is difficult and stressful to the member who is involved, is described by the leaders and main persons in some detail. The role play, which can easily be enacted within the time period of a session, involves establishing the scene, acting out the crucial elements, and exiting the scene. Then, the observers give their feedback on what has occurred, and a discussion takes place.

Leaders guide members' reactions to role-played events. The relatively safe environment of the group and friendly reactions from other members encourage shy members to try out a new way of acting. When the primary intent is for the member to discover how peers are likely to react to a novel approach, then spontaneous reactions are likely to be useful.

CHILDREN AND
ADOLESCENTS AS MEMBERS

Groups tends to be composed either of children or adolescents. Whereas children and adolescents are suitable populations for group work, the approach tends to vary somewhat for each.

Children tend to be comfortable with short sessions consisting of many brief activities. Frequently scheduled sessions are useful; ideally, no more than several days passes between sessions so that young children remember leaders they may not otherwise see.

Furthermore, as is the case with most group work with children, with the exception of classroom groups, children tend to see the other members infrequently outside of the sessions. Given that children tend to focus on the present, and given the partial development and use of memory among children, groups that meet at least weekly are preferable to those that meet less frequently.

Children may express themselves and communicate with leaders through nonverbal methods. It is important for leaders to read the emotions of the faces of young children who come to their groups. Young children are likely to make good use of movement activities as well as arts and crafts in groups, including those that make a bit of a mess! Indeed, children may be less concerned about cleanliness and appearance than their elders.

Children's cognitive development suggests the use of a concrete approach, such as showing and discussing pictures or photographs.

Repetition of material and ideas also can be useful as a summary at the end of one or a series of sessions. Presenting the same material, with different characters in a story, working with different members, or using a different medium, for example, videotape, also is effective.

Usually, parents give permission and children give their assent for group work. Particularly in the early sessions of the group, children may be determining whether and to what extent leaders are like other adults, for example, parents and teachers, whom they know. Therefore, it behooves leaders to become acquainted with the parents and teachers of the child members. Leaders wish to know whether the members have good relationships with the adults in their lives as such factors may influence trust and the development of working relationships between leaders and members in the group.

Children like to play board and computer games, musical games and instruments, and athletics, and such games are used in group work. Children tend to like and often communicate through storytelling. Stories are useful in developing the interpersonal-cognitive problem-solving skills of children. Stories give children the opportunity to think of common social situations involving other children. Children are able to relate to conflicts, dilemmas, and emotionally distressing events from a comfortable distance and gingerly to think of them and apply them to their own lives.

Leaders aim to foster the confidence of young members. They give children increasing responsibility for carrying out activities as the group develops. In other words, leadership in group work with children becomes more widely distributed over time.

Children are on their way to becoming adolescents. Nevertheless, adolescents differ from children in regard to their biological and physical, cognitive and learning, and social and emotional development. Peers take on greater significance for adolescents. Therefore, the nature of the group and its composition is likely to take on considerable significance for adolescents. Often, adolescents quickly decide about whether to be in and continue with the group.

Many adolescents tend to be emotionally sensitive and responsive to their peers. Adolescents tend to communicate well with one another in school systems. They are usually insiders with regard to the social lives of their peers in such systems. Indeed, they tend to spend considerable amounts of time out of group communicating with one another, as on the phone. As a peer group, adolescents tend to have their own language, which establishes them as a developmental cohort, characterized by or being fixed in the present, and clearly distinguishable from adults and young children.

Adolescents consider to what extent they can trust others and how much they are likely to share with others. Many adolescents tend to question authority. Therefore, leaders must be wary of assuming an authoritarian or autocratic stance within the group. Often, leaders must phrase suggestions and advice tentatively and work through other members to get messages across to members who are resistant to suggestions or advice from adults.

Adolescents are predisposed to self-disclosure. As they are still learning about intimacy, adolescents tend to have less experience than adults in regard to how much information to share in the group. Leaders guide adolescents in regard to what, how much, and when to share in the group so that it is not premature and does not become excessive, damaging, or embarrassing to the adolescent. Disclosure by adolescents should not preclude their returning to a subsequent session of the group.

Members of adolescent groups may go to extremes in regard to self-disclosure. Some adolescents may put on a self-protective front or appearance that is neither expressive nor indicative of how they are truly feeling. Several members of an adolescent group commented to Michael that he looked calm and complimented him on his ability to maintain his cool. Nonetheless, Michael was vulnerable. He felt that if anyone would look at him or say something in a certain way he would begin to cry. Indeed, during a later session, when the leader paid individualized attention to him and noticed how he was feeling, Michael did begin to cry, which embarrassed him greatly. Nevertheless, Michael returned to subsequent sessions.

Leaders should be prepared for mood swings, which tend to be common among adolescents. Stability on the part of the leader when confronted with adolescent mood swings is essential. Many adolescents are very verbal and expressive about their emotional vicissitudes. They may talk as if they are the only person who has experienced what they are feeling. Of course, the group is designed to overcome the sense of isolation that may occur in adolescence.

Whether to have mixed or single-sex groups is a controversial issue (Garvin, 1977). Mixed-sex groups tend to complicate group work with adolescents and inevitably lead to a sexual dynamic occurring among members. Whereas this type of composition can provide dynamism to the group process, leaders must be ready for patterns of attraction based on sexuality. Ryan joined an adolescent discussion group on the arts, designed to promote mental health. After several meetings of the long-term group, Ryan began approaching attractive members for dates. When several of them left the group and he did not find a girlfriend, Ryan too left the group.

Group members are likely to vary where they are in the process of approaching adulthood. Their decision-making and preferences should be respected and considered as much as possible (Garvin, 1977). Parents tend to be little involved in group work with adolescents.

Adolescents yearn for and are taking steps toward autonomy. At times, and normatively, in relation to their quest for autonomy, many adolescents have lost a considerable amount of their support from adults. In circumstances when it is difficult for adults to provide support to adolescents, their peers in and out of the group may be helpful. Nonetheless, adolescents are vulnerable to loss of support from peers. Leaders strive to be supportive in the group and to build supportive relationships among members.

Adolescents do well with activity in groups. Many tend to have a great deal of physical energy and strength. They are capable of abstract thought. Adolescents can be involved in extended practice activities, such as sophisticated role-playing strategies and scenarios, involving many people, even the entire group.

DEVELOPMENTAL PHASES

Following planning, composition, and assessment, group work tends to proceed through a series of developmental phases, each of which is associated with particular leader-initiated activities and each of which establishes the basis for and influences the subsequent phases.

Beginning Phase

The beginning phase is a pattern-setting period in which the group establishes an identity, clarifies roles, and develops norms. In many school systems and in a few small or tightly woven community systems the members already may be acquainted with one another and possibly with the leaders too. Whereas some orientation to the purpose and methods of the group begins prior to the first session, much of it takes place during the early phase. Groups with many members with little prior group work experience usually require more extensive orientation than those groups with many members with prior experience.

Norms begin to get established. The members begin to get a good idea of what is expected of them. Naming the group is useful in promoting the attractiveness and identity of the group for the members.

A natural tendency exists for a relatively high degree of disagreement to be expressed by members early in the life of the group. Nonetheless, in structured short-term groups the beginning phase and the conflicts therein tend to be less pronounced than in long-term and unstructured group work. In the beginning phase of an open-ended community recreation group, considerable conflict emerged between two preadolescent boys. The leaders used conflict resolution strategies, such as establishing separate sports for each to play, to promote harmony.

To develop the group and prevent difficulties that can interfere with the group achieving its aims, rules are set. Leaders ask members to suggest rules that then are subject to a vote. The proportion of members agreeing to adopt a rule is directly related to and is an index of its acceptance by the group.

Involving members in producing rules increases acceptance of and compliance with the rules. Children are often willing to obey rules. As adolescents customarily rebel against rules, it is essential that they are involved in creating rules that appear reasonable to them (Moss, 1992). In an early session of a community group for adolescents who had been sexually abused, the members were surprised when the leaders requested suggestions for rules. Dayna, a 15-year-old in foster care, defiantly said that the members did not need any rules! When one leader was about to respond to Dayna's statement in a confrontational manner, the other leader checked her and initiated a discussion about the value of rules in the group.

Occasionally, members lack ideas for rules. Brainstorming can be useful in such instances. The first three rules generated in a brainstorming session in a children's school performance group for third graders were (a) let us kids take over the group, (b) use less workbooks, and (c) kids decide what we want to do and what we don't want to do.

As a backup, leaders prepare a set of rules prior to the session in which rule setting is discussed. They bring in a set of rules to be modified or ratified by the members. Typical leader-based rules include the following: listen quietly; pay attention; respect everyone; don't interrupt; no punishment, hurting, or breaking. Once the rules are established and agreed to by the members they are written up in an exercise. The members write the rules on a poster board, which is displayed as a cue or reminder in subsequent sessions.

Middle and Ending Phases

Following the beginning phase the group settles its issues of leadership, power, and control, and is relatively free of conflicts that may disrupt its functioning or distract it from its work. The group then enters the middle phase, which is usually the longest and most productive phase of all. Through discussion, learning, and carrying out the activities described earlier, the group works toward achieving its aims and the members develop their problem-solving abilities.

Later in the middle phase, members are assigned leadership roles and functions on the basis of the leaders' observation and assessment of their abilities. The adult leaders determine which of the members are best suited to carry out which particular leadership roles.

For many children and adolescents, attendance patterns are directly related to parental cooperation in supporting the members and transporting them to the meeting site. In some community systems membership is likely to fluctuate considerably more than in school systems in which members are likely to remain in the group until it ends.

When a short-term group has met a predetermined number of times, or after it has accomplished its immediate objectives, it enters the ending phase. (On those occasions when the group has been unsuccessful or has not solidified, it is likely to disband early.) One of the functions of the ending phase is for the members to consolidate the gains in problem-solving skill that they have acquired in the middle phase. A review of concepts and applications, and for children playing relevant games, are means of achieving consolidation. In contrast to the beginning phase, in the ending phase leaders attempt to decrease the attractiveness and cohesion of the group and increase the attractiveness and cohesion of the external environment. Ways of ending include having a party or conducting a graduation-type ceremony.

CONCLUSION

Planning, composition, and assessment are major interrelated aspects of group work with children and adolescents that establish the basis for actual implementation in school and community systems. Questions, such as who will be in the group, what its purpose is, where and when it will meet, why the group should be established, and how it should be conducted, are the subject of planning activities. In a careful and balanced composition the use of inclusion and exclusion criteria enhances the effectiveness of group work. Assessment is an ongoing process that uses measures to consider the domain-specific functioning of individual members.

The early decisions and actions of leaders influence the life of the group. In this chapter, process has been explored in terms of useful techniques and group phases. Activities, which are tied to the developmental levels of the members, help children and adolescents cope with stress and reduce anxiety. Most activities, including role playing, involve discussion. In the following chapter the evaluation of group work will be considered.

Chapter 4

EVALUATION OF PRACTICE

Evaluations provide the basis for demonstrating the value and effects of group work. The aim of the present chapter is to provide leaders with a basis for conducting evaluations of group work with children and adolescents.

PURPOSES

The major purpose of evaluation is to provide an understanding of the immediate and long-term effects of group work on the members. Most evaluations center on the immediate effects of group work. If an effect is observed, leaders seek to determine the extent of the effect and whether it was due to group work or such factors as maturation of the youngsters. For instance, in the course of a yearlong group work program six socially isolated preadolescent girls entered puberty. The increase in popularity of four of the girls appeared to be due to the developmental changes and the group work.

At times, leaders carry out evaluations because of an administrative mandate to determine the effectiveness of the group work program. Such evaluations may be implemented to meet the accreditation requirements of the school or agency. To get ready for a report to United Way, Nadine, the director of a community service program for poor children, asked Michaela and Sarah, the leaders of a group for children with multiple problems, to describe the success of the group in attaining goals. Michaela and Sarah decided to provide a narrative account of how each child had changed in addition to an objective account based on goals that had been set and reached in the prior 3 months.

Leaders conduct evaluations to determine the impact of their practice, to discover how successful they are in conducting groups, and to demonstrate the meaningfulness and value of their work. Indeed, evaluations have the potential for revealing rewarding information to leaders.

Harry had provided group work in a community-based rehabilitation center for children and adolescents with developmental disabilities for 2 years. Although he was pleased with his work, he wished to know whether the program he used was useful. Consequently, he decided to try to evaluate the services he provided to see what impact they had on the youngsters. In conducting follow-up interviews with youngsters and their parents, Harry was pleased to discover a positive effect of his efforts with most of the groups he led.

Evaluation findings provide information and insights on the impact of the group work program, which transcend impressions derived from direct experience and involvement with the program. Formal and systematic evaluations provide objective information that complements anecdotal evidence in bolstering leaders' claims of helping members.

An important aim of evaluations is to help leaders discover and verify what is effective about their group work. Evaluations provide the basis for leaders to learn from their professional experiences. Evaluations are used to help leaders modify the process and program on the basis of systematic feedback that reveals the effective aspects of the program.

Often, the purpose of evaluation is to determine the effectiveness and efficiency of group work in preventing or resolving problems of children or adolescents. Frequently, effectiveness is the primary emphasis of the evaluation.

Nevertheless, given the expenditure of human and material resources in service design and delivery, the fiscal and administrative efficiency of the group work program in reaching the desired objectives is an important subject for evaluation.

DOMAINS AND QUESTIONS

Evaluations attempt to answer questions about the impact of group work on the problem-solving abilities, emotions and mental health, and actions and activities of the members. Indeed, the domains of evaluation include the acquisition of problem-solving knowledge and skills, which tend to be more concrete for younger children and more abstract for adolescents, and their application to situations beyond the immediate group. Interpersonal-cognitive problem-solving and family relationship skills also are important.

Asking the right questions is the key to ultimate use of the completed evaluation study (Bok, 1980). Evaluations can answer questions about the comparative success of members as they proceed through the process of group work. The process includes identification of populations-at-risk, referral, assessment, entry into the group, functioning in the group, outcome, and follow-up. Data also can be obtained from school and community service personnel regarding their perceptions of actual and ideal functions of leaders, and their awareness, use of, and satisfaction with group work (Staudt & Craft, 1983).

In addition to obtaining objective information about the effects of the group as a whole, leaders have questions related to the well-being of the members and their relationship to persons who are in and out of the group. Evaluations provide information about how and in what ways leaders and group work programs are successful in improving the well-being of the members.

PREVENTION AND INTERVENTION

Whereas extant group work programs are subject to evaluation, at times new ones are formed along with an evaluation package. For instance, at an elementary school a new group work program for improving social competence was tried out and evaluated.

Group work that emphasizes intervention is targeted at youngsters who show observable and measurable difficulties, whereas group work that emphasizes primary prevention is targeted at youngsters who may show such difficulties in the future. The evaluation of group work programs includes a measurement of the acquisition and application of problem-solving concepts and skills. Nevertheless, the implementation of evaluation of group work frequently is more feasible in intervention programs than in primary prevention programs. That is, the effects of the former are sometimes more demonstrable than those of the latter. The evaluation of the effectiveness of primary prevention programs requires a long-term follow-up to determine how many youngsters actually developed what kinds of difficulties at what levels of seriousness.

Evaluation usually involves a comparison of the functioning of youngsters who received group work with those who received another intervention, delayed intervention, or the usual level of service. A related comparison is that of the characteristics of youngsters who presently have or who recently had difficulties with well-functioning youngsters.

Evaluation of groups consists of a consideration of their structure and functioning and their attractiveness and cohesiveness. Evaluation of individual members is an estimation of process and outcome, that is, how members have improved in their functioning, as in their attendance, participation, and success in reaching individualized objectives. The attainment of objectives by members and groups is directly related.

Evaluation involves an examination of functioning of members within school and community systems. Evaluation of members of groups in school systems includes a consideration of their school performance, whereas members of groups in community systems tend to be evaluated in regard to both their school performance and community behaviors.

Leaders and members are bound together in an activity pattern within the group that leads to particular outcomes. The evaluation may include the leaders, the members, and the group work program. Measurement of the performance of the leaders involves examining the groups that they have led. Measurement of the members involves examining their functioning inside and outside the group.

Group work programs have value on two levels, one of which is that they provide services that are available to populations of children and adolescents. An additional factor is the demonstrated effect of the program. An effective and appropriate program delivered by capable leaders is likely to have a beneficial effect on the members. When it is demonstrated that many youngsters have benefited from the program, then rewards may come to those who are involved with delivering and evaluating the program.

Furthermore, power aspects of evaluation are important considerations in demonstrating the value of a given program of group work with children and adolescents (Bok, 1980). Steps are taken to promote confidence in and understanding of evaluation processes and products. For instance, at the annual meeting of the board of directors of a community mental health center the evaluation results were presented for subsequent public relations purposes. It was shown that 75% of the adolescents who participated improved somewhat or very much.

AGENTS

Within the school or community, agency evaluations often are conducted by the leaders. Indeed, leaders often are called on to evaluate their own performance, even as a component of an evaluation conducted by external professional evaluators.

Occasionally, evaluations of group work are conducted by evaluation teams or units in which the team members collect the data under guidance, direction, and supervision.

When the evaluators are persons other than the leaders themselves, an orientation meeting should be held with those leaders whose group work program is being evaluated. The briefing and a question-and-answer session allows for an explanation of procedures. A basis for a cooperative relationship between evaluators and leaders is established. The evaluation team meets with those who participate in the evaluation, including the members.

Concerns of leaders who are wary of external evaluations may be addressed on two levels. One, it is incumbent on the evaluator to establish a proper relationship with the leader whose group is being evaluated. Two, the evaluator seeks to maximize the sensitivity of the instruments, the power of the statistical tests, and the adequacy of the evaluation design to detect differences or change that actually are present.

Whereas evaluations are meant to be objective, the persons conducting the evaluation may have expectations to find either positive or negative outcomes, which may influence the results of the evaluation. Persons who seek to find meaningful results, namely that the program worked, and who have an investment in the program, tend to have positive expectations. Persons who have doubts about the program and wish to scrutinize it, tend to have negative expectations. If leaders sense that the evaluators are critical or negative, then some defensiveness or resistance may develop toward the evaluator, which, ironically, will take some problem-solving skill to deflect. To control for such factors and promote objectivity, an attempt usually is made to achieve some distance between the persons who design, conduct, and are participants of the evaluation. Maintaining a role differentiation between leaders and evaluators has the advantage of providing an objective view, which reduces the probability of passing along evaluators' expectations and biasing evaluation results.

TYPES

Composition, process, and outcome evaluations are planned and implemented. Composition evaluations are performed to compose groups. The characteristics of potential members are noted and considered in assembling groups.

Process evaluations describe the functioning of extant groups as they move to meet their objectives. Such evaluations include analyses of how group work is influenced by the leaders and the changes in such variables as social status, attendance, participation, satisfaction, and emotional well-being among the members from session to session.

Timely process evaluations can forestall difficulties that might jeopardize the success of groups. In calling attention to areas of function and dysfunction in groups at particular time periods, such as levels of cohesion, communication, and conflict in beginning, middle, and ending phases, process evaluations may lead to correction of process. For example, in the middle phase of a group held at a university-based community research center the evaluator noted the levels of leadership and member participation in activities. The evaluator informed the leader of a decline in participation of members in the observer role of the role-play situations. The leader acted quickly to improve the situation.

Outcome evaluations are the most important type of evaluations for advancing knowledge about the effectiveness of group work. Outcome evaluations indicate the results and effectiveness of group work and thereby influence agency policy and program. For instance, at a community mental health center, an outcome evaluation showed that the adolescent members of an aftercare group had a greater degree of success in reaching their individual objectives than other clients. Consequently, the agency treatment policy team recommended an expansion of the adolescent aftercare group work program.

Outcome evaluations encompass the definition of a problem, the identification of the group work method used to resolve the problem, the desired outcome, and the criteria for determining the attainment of the desired outcome. Outcome evaluations consist of two types: formative and summative. Formative or ongoing evaluations are used to contribute to a longer-term assessment of the impact and value of group work. Formative evaluation of group work with children and adolescents provides information about its effectiveness prior to its conclusion and is a source of feedback to social systems. An example of a formative evaluation is an interim report of progress toward reaching individualized objectives of the members.

Process evaluations contribute to the creation of formative evaluations. In the absence of a formal formative evaluation, process information illustrates progress about the means or process that ultimately leads to the ends or outcome. For example, in a group of young children the leader learned that many tended to be distracted and had a difficult time focusing on the activities. The process evaluation suggested that the members could be making better use of the group.

Summative outcome evaluations provide a definitive indicator of the results of group work and encompass final decision making about impact and value. Such evaluations appraise the functioning of members at the conclusion of the program. The maintenance of change that has been achieved is reported in the summative outcome evaluation. Often, the examination of the status of members following the end of the group is accomplished by collecting data that are parallel to those collected at the beginning.

As quantitative evaluations tend to have considerable credibility to administrators, researchers, academicians, and policymakers, it is important for leaders who wish to demonstrate program effectiveness to consider using such methods. Such methods include the administration of inventories that lend themselves to quantification. Single-system designs are useful ways of measuring change within the member or group, and group comparison experimental designs make use of comparison, control, or both groups (Meares, 1980).

Quantitative methods are used to precisely record and statistically analyze changes in the characteristics of the members as well as group functions. Statistical analyses range from simple frequency distributions to multivariate statistics.

Cognitions that are measured include various aspects of problem solving, such as means-ends problem-solving thinking (see LeCroy, 1986). Alternative thinking is measured in an interview in which problematic social situations are presented. The member responds to the evaluator's probes, which are designed to elicit the maximum number of alternatives (Platt, Spivack, Altman, Altman, & Piezzer, 1974; Spivack & Levine, 1973; Spivack et al., 1976). The evaluation of consequential thinking also involves the evaluator presenting problematic social situations that are appropriate to the developmental level of the member. In the interview, the member describes potential consequences of a situationally based action, such as a provocation (Platt, Spivack, & Bloom, 1971; Walter & Peters, 1980).

Qualitative evaluations rely on the gathering of in-depth information to broadly describe changes of the members. Such information is ordinarily collected through an interview process that allows the member to speak freely on a specified topic. Through a categorization of ideas, the collected data then are analyzed for commonalities of responses and interpreted. Evaluation interviews, which are low in structure and formality, and are often qualitative, are often exploratory in nature.

In contrast, interviews that are high in structure and formality, and are often quantitative, are often part of more rigorous evaluation designs that may include a comparative or control group in a quasi-experiment or experiment. To allow for a range of complementary information to be gathered, one statistical, another narrative, a combination of quantitative and qualitative methodologies sometimes is used as part of process and outcome evaluations. For example, in the process evaluation of group work aimed at promoting the health of urban adolescents process recordings made by one set of leaders complemented the closed-ended questionnaires that their co-leaders completed following each session.

COMPLEXITY

Evaluations of group work vary in scale and complexity. Some evaluations are conducted as part of a larger multisite outcome study. For example, a study was planned to test the effectiveness of group work in several regions.

Some evaluations are conducted as part of a study of the effectiveness of a multicomponent system of service delivery. For instance, a study involved a comparison of the effectiveness of individual, family, and group approaches to helping adolescents with substance abuse disorders.

The multiple goals of many schools and community agencies tends to complicate the evaluation process (Witkin, Shapiro, & McCall, 1980). Whereas evaluation of groups that deal with a central problem is relatively simple, evaluation of groups that have members with multiple problems is of course more complex and centers on each of several problems and their interaction.

Indeed, the evaluation of multiple problems requires multivariate methods to tease out the contribution of each problem to overall distress and dysfunction.

CONDUCT AND MEASURES

Leaders complete the design of the evaluation, including the measurement of variables, prior to data collection and prior to the sessions. As such, design precedes and determines implementation.

Many evaluation projects are designed to ascertain the relationship between process and outcome through data collection. Process data include member attendance, participation in activities, and satisfaction. In regard to functioning of members, outcome data include problem resolution. The measurement of group level variables, such as cohesion, describe how groups function and influence the members. Evaluation involves sampling and examining a small number of variables. Data from individual members can be combined to inform leaders about how the group is functioning.

For such practical purposes as composing the group, and to determine the value and impact of group work, evaluation involves the application of measurement procedures, methods, and tools or instruments. Data collection involves briefly explaining and administering particular instruments, including their confidential aspects.

Using reports of sessions, leaders record and report process and outcome information. Forms are used to standardize the gathering of information. A review of records for consistency and completeness helps assure high quality data collection.

Leaders collect some evaluation data in an explicit and noticeable manner. In a high school group, the members knew when the leaders asked them for social information about their relationships to peers.

Leaders also may collect data about functioning in school and community systems in a less reactive manner. Unobtrusive measures of functioning include school grade point averages and attendance records and community arrest and institutionalization reports.

Leaders obtain the members' perspective on changes that they have experienced on a variety of measures. Self-reports include paper-and-pencil tests and inventories of performance in social situations. As an alternative to the more traditional paper-and-pencil tests, role-play tests provide a useful albeit small sample of children's social performance in simulated situations. Role-play tests involve the leaders and members each enacting a role in a simulated social situation. Some role-play tests address initial reactions and responses within particular social situations.

The perspective of those who have an opportunity to observe and interact with youngsters is valuable. Through naturalistic observation of youngsters in school and community systems, many leaders have the opportunity to obtain a useful view of their social activity.

Evaluations provide leaders with the views of those persons whose expectations ultimately must be met. Adults form judgments of youngsters, which subsequently influence the latter's adjustment in school and community systems. The perceptions of leaders, members, peers, classmates, friends, teachers, administrators, and family members are gathered through interviews and recorded in inventories.

Leaders may interview administrators to determine their perceptions of the success of group work, based on formal evaluation reports as well as informal feedback that they have received. Through their observations and relationships, children and adolescents often provide valuable insights into the social status and sociability of their peers. The perspective of peers in the classroom and neighborhood of members aids leaders in evaluating the members' social relationships. The peer perspective is ordinarily measured at several data points, including, at a minimum, prior to and soon following the end of the series of group work sessions.

Sociometry, which maps out the web of attractions within known social groups, provides the basis for improving members' interpersonal and intergroup relations. Leaders use sociometry to understand changes in the social statuses of popular, average, isolated, neglected, and rejected youngsters among their peers.

One useful version of the sociometric technique is the peer roster-and-rating measure, which involves the collection of the names of youngsters within the child's peer or social group. The technique involves asking youngsters a sociometric question, such as, "How much do you like to play with this child in school?" After the rating forms are distributed to the youngsters and the data are collected, they are analyzed by compiling the nominations given and received by each child. Differences are determined within and between individuals and groups across time.

Structured observations by adults are useful in measuring the level and kind of members' peer interaction. Trained adults are able to make sufficiently reliable and valid observations.

Teachers are in a very good position to observe the task-oriented and playful social activities of their pupils. They observe youngsters in class working on their own as well as doing task-oriented work in small and large groups. Teachers observe youngsters at play with peers in the school environment, including the playground.

Teachers have a perspective based on large numbers of pupils with whom they interact. The seniority and experience of teachers influences their reference unit for considering and comparing the adjustment, performance, and interaction of particular youngsters. Teachers usually have a good idea of what constitutes normal and appropriate functioning for school-age youngsters.

Like teachers, pupil personnel team members are in a good position to observe and compare normal and average levels and kinds of social activity among school-age children. On the basis of their observations, pupil-personnel-service team members complete measures and write reports.

Outside consultants to schools also function as observers. Mental health professionals are frequently requested to observe youngsters in the classroom and in naturalistic settings, such as the playground.

When group work is conducted in the schools with youngsters who are having difficulties in classrooms, an evaluation that includes the classroom is warranted. Such an evaluation reveals relationship patterns and the social status of individuals and groups within the classroom. A comprehensive evaluation, which requires the efforts of an evaluation team, encompasses multiple screening of all children in the class and the use of measures of teacher perceptions of the classroom environment, measures of class perceptions of the teacher, observer ratings of classroom interaction, and sociometric instruments.

At times, school-based observations are complemented by systematic parental observations. Whereas many parents are subjective observers of their children, they can be trained to make objective observations.

In community mental health agencies, measures are used to assess youngsters' psychopathology in relation to a larger population of youngsters. Multiple perspectives indicate who perceives children as having what kinds and levels of problems. Related forms of the Child Behavior Checklist, a well-validated measure, are available for completion by teachers, parents, and the youngsters (Achenbach, 1982).

Occasionally, leaders desire information that transcends the customary focus of evaluation. Measures of locus of control, which indicate how youngsters attribute or explain events, provide leaders with a basis for understanding members. Self-concept measures are useful in determining how the youngsters perceive themselves and assessing to what extent self-concept is a problem area to be addressed in the group.

Regular monitoring of members by leaders is helpful for determining changes in their functioning and in gauging the external and internal states, such as anxiety, of members as well as the processes and outcomes of group work. The resolution of problems is measurable through goal attainment scaling (G.A.S.), an evaluation tool that complements substantive measures of such constructs as psychopathology (Kiresuk & Sherman, 1968, 1977). The G.A.S. is useful in conducting systematic evaluations and determining the progress of individuals and groups toward attaining objectives.

Subsequent to collecting and analyzing data, leaders compare evaluation data that have been obtained from members, youngsters in comparison groups, and, if available, national age-referenced peer norms. Each of the comparisons has distinctive value. By comparing the data obtained with data that were collected from the same youngsters at a prior time period, such as baseline, leaders see how members have changed. By comparing the data with that obtained from other youngsters who are members of the same group, leaders determine how individuals fare in comparison to their group. By comparing the data to peers who are in other groups and who share another social context within the school or community system, leaders assess members' standing in regard to peer society.

By making comparisons with national age-referenced peer norms and using nationally normed tests, such as the Pittsburgh Adjustment Survey Scales (Ross, Lacey, & Parton, 1965) and the School Behavior Checklist (Miller, 1972), leaders gauge the statistical normality of characteristics of the members.

TIMING AND PROCESS

In a sense, leaders begin the evaluation process by attaining the consent to deliver the group work program. Prior to conducting evaluations, leaders request approval from administrators for their evaluation procedures (Wiggins & Moody, 1987). Administrators who have an investment in, and a series of successful and beneficial experiences with, evaluation may readily approve it. Authorities at the local level may have their actions approved at the district or regional level. Ideally, the evaluation process becomes incorporated within the school or community agency as a regular set of procedures accompanying the regular use of group work.

The timing of the evaluation, which includes when and how frequently the data collection occurs, is related to the type and method of evaluation. Process evaluations involve frequent data collection during and between each session. In outcome evaluations, data collection tends to occur less frequently and may include the use of rapid assessment instruments as well as measures that may take longer to complete (Corcoran & Fischer, 1987).

In planning the evaluation, the leaders establish the time frame, including the option for a follow-up evaluation. Time periods for data collection include the intervals before, during, after, and as a follow-up to the group work.

Leaders compare the functioning of members at different times, for instance, from the beginning of the group until its conclusion. Measurements occur at two or more intervals.

Leaders consider the tolerance and time that the group can devote to data collection. At times, leaders devote one pregroup session and one postgroup session to data collection. After the group has started to meet, a brief period within, and often at the end of, each session is devoted to data collection. Frequently, leaders, members, and observers collect data within sessions.

Some leaders conduct a short-term follow-up evaluation several weeks, or at most a few months, after the group has ended. Occasionally, leaders are interested in conducting long-term follow-up studies. Leaders who plan to conduct a long-term follow-up should maintain regular communication with members, including contacting them annually, organizing additional meetings, and conducting yearly evaluations. Leaders who keep good records of members and make efforts to track them within and across school and community systems may find it feasible to conduct long-term follow-up studies.

Leaders determine who will conduct the evaluation, what kinds of data will be collected, and how the data will be analyzed. Leaders select measures that are appropriate for the age group, reading level, and social-emotional developmental level of the members. Ordinarily, leaders use multiple measures to provide several views on process and outcome and to overcome the limitations of any one measure.

In large-scale evaluation projects, leaders work with an evaluation team. They orient staff as to the purpose of the evaluation and the nature and characteristics of the instruments. Leaders orient and train assistants to carry out the tasks of the evaluation and explain how procedures are implemented and forms are completed. By simulating the completion of forms with persons who play the role of respondents, the evaluation team learns how to administer the instruments before they are used with the members.

Leaders anticipate potential obstacles, including children or adolescents and staff being absent and unavailable for participation in the evaluation on a given day, due to such factors as illness, sudden changes in school or agency schedules, and loss or spoilage of supplies. A certain amount of flexibility and the availability of backup staff and supplies will see most leaders through most such obstacles.

Leaders activate procedures for maintaining confidentiality by using locked and secure files and code names and numbering systems that safeguard the identity of individuals and groups. They arrange to organize, code, and prepare the stored and protected data for computerized analysis. For some instruments, the leaders mail the raw data, namely the completed forms, to the publisher who returns the analyzed results to the leaders.

The leaders derive the results of the evaluation and draw their conclusions. In some instances the evaluation results will make the group work program appear well. Nevertheless, evaluation results may convey differences in effectiveness among group work programs, between the group work program and other types of practice, between practice settings, or even between leaders. Such findings must be handled with the care.

The leaders prepare a written copy of the report, which includes tables of data and narratives. They present the report to personnel in the school or community system and conduct a discussion session. Subsequently, they may revise the report and distribute it more widely.

AN EXAMPLE:
OUI ARE FRIENDS

A practitioner led a social competence group to promote the development of interpersonal-cognitive problem-solving (ICPS) skills for fourth-grade students in an elementary school. The children originally called the group "We are Friends" and changed it to "Oui are Friends" when a French-speaking girl joined the group. The leader had a positive and longstanding professional relationship with many of the teachers in the school. The leader had offered ICPS groups twice before to children in the same school and, on observing the members and talking to teachers following each series, had the impression that the groups had a favorable impact on the attitudes and well-being of the members. The leader had obtained anecdotal evidence of the value of the first series of ICPS groups.

In the second series of such groups he began exploring the use of instruments to potentially provide additional, complementary evidence of the impact and value of such groups. The leader tried out several self-report measures to determine to what extent the members understood and were comfortable with the measures, to see how useful the measures might be in gauging changes in the members, and to refine his own skills in administering the measures.

In this third series of ICPS groups the leader wished to take his plans for evaluation a step further by implementing a more extensive evaluation. Fortunately, he had the approval of his supervisor to devote additional resources of time and effort to his evaluation project. She saw that he had the potential to further the application of program evaluation designs within the school system.

For the ICPS groups the leader wished to assess how well the children were developing their social competencies and to what extent others were noticing changes in the school. The leader decided to measure the effects of the group on the acquisition of the ICPS skills and to determine to what extent changes in social behavior were observed in the classrooms by the teachers of the children in the group.

The leader selected two available measures that were suggested by a school psychologist, who was a member of the pupil personnel staff.

The School Behavior Checklist (SBC; Miller, 1972) included 11 global judgment items and 96 items that described children's behaviors. The SBC had Low Need Achievement (LNA), Aggression (AGG), Anxiety (ANX), Academic Disability (AD), Hostile Isolation (HI), Extroversion (EXT), and Total Disability (TD) scales.

The Children's Means-Ends Problem-Solving (C-MEPS) instrument (Shure & Spivack, 1972) consisted of six stories for which the leader supplied the beginnings and ends and the youngsters created the middles. For instance, one story centers around a child who spends time with other children when one of them says something unpleasant to the child, who subsequently becomes angry and seeks revenge. The story ends with the child happy about settling the score. The leader wrote down each story recounted by the child and later tallied the number of means plus the number of obstacles plus the number of indications of time to arrive at a total means-ends problem-solving score. Higher scores indicated greater means-ends problem-solving ability.

The leader wished to see whether there was any change that occurred during the life of the group. Consequently, he decided to administer the measures immediately before the sessions began and immediately after they concluded. Prior to administering the measures or beginning the group sessions, the leader held a training session to explain the SBC to the classroom teachers. As requested, the teachers agreed to complete the SBC twice and despite many demands on their time the teachers managed to complete the forms. The leader decided to administer the C-MEPS during individual pregroup and postgroup interviews, which he held with all 11 members.

In addition to assessing the outcome of the group in regard to members' problem-solving skills and social behaviors, the leader also gathered information while the group was underway to help guide its process. Toward the end of each group session, each member completed a brief satisfaction measure. Members were given a choice of adjectives, that is, happy, sad, mad, and glad, and circled the one that designated how they mostly felt about the session.

To help plan succeeding group sessions as well as to learn from the entire set of sessions and plan the next set of ICPS groups, the leader decided to keep a record of his own view of group process. Immediately following each session he completed a two-page inventory pertaining to the process of the group, including the names of the members, their attendance, promptness in attendance, satisfaction levels, participation in activities, difficulties noted by the leader, and proposed solutions. The inventory served as a problem-solving tool for the leader.

The results on the SBC provided a variegated picture of the social functioning of each member in the school at two points in time. Whereas some members improved on each scale, improvements were noted for most members on the AGG, ANX, and TD scales. These results implied that teachers noted an overall improvement for most children as well as reductions in aggression and anxiety in the classroom.

Results from the SBC were available for individual members too. For instance, Jenny's teacher noted global and overall changes in her social behavior in the classroom as well as in a wider range of specific areas than tended to be observed for most other members. On 10 of the global items of the SBC, Jenny was rated by her teacher as being an average child. On the remaining global item, her teacher rated her as being more likeable or appealing than average. Whereas Jenny remained about the same on the LNA, AD, and EXT scales after the group as she had before the group, an improvement was noted on the AGG, ANX, HI, and TD scales.

The results on the C-MEPS provided both qualitative and quantitative information on each member prior to and following the group. Overall, the number of obstacles that were assessed in members' stories increased most, followed by the numbers of means. The number of indications of time for the group as a whole was virtually unchanged. Such results suggested that the members became sensitized to the existence of interpersonal problems during the course of the group.

One C-MEPS story begins with a child breaking her mother's flower pot. The youngster anticipates her mother's anger and ends with her mother acting kindly toward her. Jenny's response following the group was as follows: "He broke it with his basketball. His brothers and sisters helped him put it back together. He bought his mother flowers and when he put them in, water came out of the holes. She had a new one and didn't mind." Jenny's total means-ends problem-solving score and its three components all increased from the first to second administration of the measure suggesting that she gained in comprehensive aspects of means-ends problem solving.

The process measure completed by the members indicated that satisfaction remained high throughout most of the sessions. Nevertheless, the youngsters were least happy with the third session, for which the leader was inadequately prepared owing to a crisis in his marriage. Jenny circled the adjective indicating that she was happy with the group for 10 of the 12 sessions too.

The leader's inventory indicated that 9 of the 11 members attended 11 or more of the sessions. Such good attendance patterns were expected given that the group met at the school. Furthermore, 8 of the members were prompt, that is, they arrived within 5 minutes of the starting time, for 10 or more sessions. Only two members were unwilling to participate in role-playing activities during the first four sessions. Nevertheless, after that point only one member refrained from such participation. That member gained very little according to the SBC and C-MEPS. Jenny attended all but two sessions and was prompt at all sessions she attended. Like most of the members, she engaged in all activities.

The leader's inventory sensitized the leader to group difficulties and allowed the leader to gain a good sense of what worked best in actually conducting the group. One difficulty that emerged in the group was noted in sessions in which two hypothetical situations were presented to the members. The attention to and quality of discussion was dramatically reduced in the second hypothetical situation. On the basis of using the inventory the leader decided to limit the number of discussions of hypothetical situations to one per session.

Whereas the leader was aware that the evaluation represented progress over the one that was conducted in the prior sequence of ICPS groups, he also recognized that the evaluation had its limitations. He realized that the results that were obtained could have been due to events external to the group. Indeed, shortly after the group began, three of the members enrolled in a bowling team, which potentially may have added to their social competence. The leader also recognized that the teachers' ratings may have been somewhat biased in favor of children whom they liked. To reduce biased expectations, the leader wished that the teachers were "blind" to whether and which children received group work. Furthermore, as it was not feasible for the leader to conduct a controlled study, the evaluation did not allow the leader to definitively determine what had caused the changes that were observed.

Nevertheless, the leader was satisfied that some desirable changes appeared to occur for group members. Many members improved important aspects of their school behavior and interpersonal-cognitive problem-solving skills. Most appeared to be satisfied with the group. The leader was pleased that he was able to observe and gather information that went beyond his own personal observations and insights. Although using the instruments had demanded extra time and effort, which had reduced the amount of time he had been able to spend with his young family, he felt it was worthwhile. Indeed, he even used the evaluation findings to bolster his own annual performance evaluation!

CONCLUSION

Several types of evaluations are germane to group work. This chapter has focused on leaders conducting composition, process, and outcome evaluations. Leaders usually want to know how to form a group, to understand more about what is happening during the course of the group, and to understand the impact of group work on the children and adolescents who are members. By working with members, peers, family members, and agency and school administrators and staff, leaders may find answers to these and related questions.

Chapter 5

A REVIEW OF THE FIELD

Group work with children and adolescents in school and community systems is a substantial and expanding field of practice that represents an application of more widely used theories and models. Many groups for children and adolescents are theme oriented. For instance, many primary prevention groups cover a range of topics that reflect concerns common to the ages of the members. Furthermore, certain domains of knowledge, for example, developmental psychopathology, are particularly useful for particular types of groups, for example, mental health. The purpose of this chapter is to provide an analysis of group work with children and adolescents, including its effectiveness, and offer recommendations for the development of practice.

A SOCIAL
PROBLEM-SOLVING APPROACH

Group work for helping children and adolescents relies considerably on structured activity and allows members to work together toward reaching common, limited objectives and solving shared problems. Cooperative activity is useful in helping children and adolescents function better in social groups. Some of the major findings from preventive and interventive group work practice point to the value of highly organized, well-planned efforts at skill provision and social support.

Group work emphasizes the assessment, prevention, and resolution of members' social problems. A creative framework consisting of three major components is useful in providing the opportunity for members to cope with and resolve social problems (Treffinger, 1995). The framework, which is partially applicable to young children, can be fully used in group work with adolescents.

First, in understanding the problem, participants discuss ambiguous challenges and concerns and consider facts, opinions, impressions, concerns, paradoxes, and circumstances. Second, participants seek specific questions and, in generating problem statements and ideas, use fluent, flexible, original, and elaborative thinking patterns. Third, in planning for action, participants examine promising options closely to determine what steps will be taken, undertake a search for assistance, and overcome potential sources of resistance.

Creative uses of problem solving that transcend the individual member, the group, and time limitations also are feasible. For instance, some youngsters may concurrently be members of multiple groups. Furthermore, it is sometimes feasible for members to participate in a succession of increasingly advanced groups over an extended period of time as they develop from childhood through adolescence. Broadening practice to include work with multiple groups also can be helpful. Involving the entire school system or additional components of the community system can increase the acquisition of problem-solving skills.

APPLICATIONS
OF GROUP WORK

Group work is designed to help children and adolescents who potentially or actually manifest social problems that invariably also have a significant impact on their families and neighbors. Social problems stemming from the members' social environment, such as parental divorce, and problems in functioning, such as social competence, have the potential to affect members' school performance and achievement levels.

The social and emotional impact of divorce has contributed to the widespread use of group work in school systems. Nevertheless, whereas divorce continues to have a major deleterious impact on many members, a rational allocation of effort suggests that greater attention be paid to the use of group work to help members develop their social competence. A contributing relationship appears to exist between low levels of parental social competence and their divorce and between the social competence of parents and that of their children. Members are likely to benefit from their participation in group work by a gain in social competence.

The social competence of members contributes to their life adjustment and is worthy of active encouragement by leaders. As the significance and consequences of social competence become more widely known, schools are more likely to attend to its development. Just as academic abilities and achievement are currently assessed on a regular basis in most school systems, so may the assessment of social competence become routinized. Such assessments, which could be performed routinely and relatively unobtrusively, would provide a portrait of the functioning of children and adolescents in their classes and grades and would be useful in planning group work.

Furthermore, extant social competence group work can be modified. Social skills training and interpersonal-cognitive problem-solving programs can be effectively combined (LeCroy & S. D. Rose, 1986). Whereas feelings are often the subject of social competence programs, as in affective education, they are also often placed in a minor position. The role of emotion, which is an indicator of success, requires greater emphasis in group work.

The prevalence of social competence deficits and mental and substance abuse disorders among school-age children and adolescents creates a demand for group work (LeCroy, 1992). Group work can continue to improve the chances of members for future social, school, and occupational success. Social competence programs can be tailored for members diagnosed with mental disorders.

Carefully composed preventive and interventive groups can help members perform better academically. New cooperative structures and arrangements between the academic and pupil personnel areas within school systems and among the family, school, and community are possible in the future.

GROUP WORK IN SCHOOL
AND COMMUNITY SYSTEMS

Children and adolescents are socialized within school and community systems and are influenced by small and large educational and social groups. The meaning and influence of the peer group is demonstrably larger for adolescents than for children. Social and recreational groups often are organized around special interests.

In community systems, group work reflects its agency auspices. Furthermore, in many communities children are involved in informal playground and neighborhood groups. They are also often members of formally organized groups affiliated with scouting and with religious institutions.

In community systems, group work, which is sometimes skill oriented, is usually substantially concerned with family and mental health issues. Personality changes are frequently the focus of therapeutic group work in community mental health agencies.

In school systems, group work tends to be educational in focus and character. Group work in school systems is designed to address the social and academic functioning of members. Many school-based groups contain members who have physical, mental, or substance abuse disorders. School-based groups for children and adolescents with mental and substance abuse disorders often retain a focus on achievement and academic performance.

Group work in schools, which is often a component of social-emotional education and more traditional educational areas, is frequently located within and corresponds directly to a curriculum area, such as social studies. Cooperation from and involvement of educational staff, including teachers, as agents of referral and as coleaders is important for ensuring the success of the group.

In-grade educational and psychological assessments of children and adolescents are routinely implemented in schools. Youngsters who are identified as having special abilities are likely to be further assessed. Difficulties that are assessed early can be addressed early through group work.

Teachers, pupil-personnel-service practitioners, administrators, staff, and classmates provide the social context for referral to and change within groups in school systems. Neighbors, friends, and acquaintances of members often relate to the focus of groups in community systems. Many of these persons have differing perceptions of the difficulties faced by members and how they can best be alleviated. When they are in agreement about the importance of group work for particular members, practice is likely to proceed smoothly. Nonetheless, when disagreement exists, it is often up to the leaders to bring about collaboration and understanding and to reduce conflict. Whereas adults substantially define the problems of children and adolescents, the views of members as well as of their peers substantially influence the presentation and definition of such problems, and discussions of such matters are an important part of the process of group work.

Preventive and interventive group work is designed for maximum applicability. The materials, duration, activity, and setting of group work are closely related to group processes within school and community systems.

STUDIES OF EFFECTIVENESS

The importance of evaluation and research pertaining to group work with children and adolescents in school and community systems has been recognized for many years (Cohen, 1967). Research on group work with children and adolescents has become more sophisticated.

How effective are various types of applied groups? Accumulated anecdotal evidence, which supports the value of divorce groups in school systems, can be considered in many ways (Cole & Kammer, 1984; Farmer & Galaris, 1993; Hoffman, 1984). For instance, many children appear to enjoy such groups. Some anecdotal evidence suggests that group work can protect children's self-esteem, which is challenged when they harbor angry feelings toward absent parents (Pfeifer & Abrams, 1984).

Empirical studies have shown that multimodal groups are effective in changing attitudes of children toward divorce and improving their classroom conduct (Anderson, Kinney, & Gerler, 1984). Programmatic group work projects have shown encouraging results. The Children's Support Group Program of the Divorce Adjustment Project has been shown to improve the self-concept and social skills of 7- to 13-year-old children (Stolberg & Garrison, 1985). Children of Divorce Intervention Program (CODIP) groups have been shown to be effective in helping children and adolescents cope with the stressful social-emotional sequelae of divorce (Alpert-Gillis, Pedro-Carroll, & Cowen, 1989; Pedro-Carroll, Alpert-Gillis, & Cowen, 1992; Pedro-Carroll, Cowen, & Gillis, 1989). Research studies have shown the effects of school-based, child-focused, supportive problem-solving group work with urban children in improved home and school adjustment, reductions in divorce-related concerns, and greater competence (Cowen et al., 1989). Additional research studies showed that late latency suburban children of divorce had significant improvements in such areas as overall adjustment, communication, openness in sharing feelings, age-appropriate activity, ability to deal with problematic situations, reduced anxiety, and acceptance and understanding of family changes, as judged by ratings of teachers, parents, children, and leaders (Pedro-Carroll & Cowen, 1985; Pedro-Carroll, Cowen, Hightower & Guare, 1986).

Additional empirical studies have shown the beneficial impact of group work on particular areas of functioning of children of divorce. For instance, group work was shown to be successful in raising the academic competence of sixth-grade children (Crosbie-Burnett & Newcomer, 1990).

Evidence tends to be favorable about the effectiveness of group work in helping children with the emotional sequelae of divorce. One study showed the effectiveness of a divorce group in reducing depression, anxiety, and negative feelings about divorce among children ages 9 to 11 (Gwynn & Brantley, 1987). At least two studies have shown that group work can positively influence the self-concept of children of divorce (Omizo & Omizo, 1987, 1988). In another empirical study, parents whose fourth- and fifth-grade children participated in group work reported that the children were less distractible, had fewer disturbed peer relations, were less immature, and overall had fewer behavior problems (Tedder, Scherman, & Wantz, 1987).

Although most empirical studies have clearly shown the effectiveness of group work with children of divorce, some empirical studies revealed only modest results (Bornstein, Bornstein, & Walters, 1988). Furthermore, some studies have not shown its effectiveness (Kalter, Pickar, & Lesowitz, 1984). One study failed to demonstrate improvement in anxiety and self-esteem for children of divorce in group counseling programs (Hett & Rose, 1991). Another study failed to show significant treatment effects for divorce groups with third- and fourth-grade elementary school children (Boren, 1983).

The effects of group work on children and adolescents with social competence difficulties also have been the focus of empirical research. Modeling and role play have been shown to be effective in improving the abilities of urban high school students to think adaptively of ways to solve problems and to perform more effectively in self-presentation situations (Sarason & Sarason, 1981). Some evidence exists for the effectiveness of groups designed to enhance either the interpersonal-cognitive problem-solving skills or the social skills of children and adolescents. Several studies support claims for the feasibility and effectiveness of preventive and interventive group work in public and parochial school systems (Rose, 1985, 1986). A research study showed the effectiveness of structured group work in teaching problem-solving skills to acting-out adolescent girls in junior high school (de Anda, 1985).

Group assertiveness training has been shown to be useful in reducing adolescent aggression (Huey, 1983), improving the ability of junior high school students to make refusal statements (McCullagh, 1981), and bettering the overall social adjustment of shy children to school, including increasing their assertiveness and self-esteem (Leone & Gumaer, 1979). Another study supported the effectiveness of group social skills training in improving the social actions of children in grades three to five with their peers (LaGreca & Santogrossi, 1980). An additional study showed that group work emphasizing conversational skills with peers, joining ongoing activities, and including others in one's activities resulted in significant improvements on a posttest role-play test and follow-up sociometric ratings (Hepler & Rose, 1988). Low social status or rejected children showed significant improvements on a posttest role-play test and a follow-up improvement on negative peer nominations. Anecdotal and empirical evidence support the value and effectiveness of group work for promoting the mental health of children and adolescents. One empirical research study showed that an activity-based group reduced anxiety and improved self-esteem (Richert, 1986). In several studies, changes immediately following group work differed from those at follow-up. One such study showed a short-term effect, which did not persist long-term, in reducing disciplinary problems in the classroom for behaviorally disturbed adolescents (Rauch, Brack, & Orr, 1987). In another study, depressed adolescents who participated in a therapeutic support group initially showed greater improvements in regard to depression and self-concept than those who participated in a social skills training group (Fine, Forth, Gilbert, & Haley, 1991). A follow-up revealed that both maintained an improvement in functioning and that the latter caught up with the former.

Mental health and substance abuse group work may improve members' problem solving. Anecdotal evidence from one report suggested that application of the mutual aid model results in most adolescent members participating in group decision making, which is followed by a reduction in their use of psychoactive substances (Gallagher, 1983).

In addition to anecdotal evidence (Brown & Papagno, 1991), empirical research studies have been conducted on the use of group work to improve school performance. Many such studies have been encouraging. A pilot study showed that the attitudes toward school and learning of retained primary grade children who received group work improved (Campbell & Bowman, 1993). Another study showed the usefulness of a marathon group approach in improving school attitude and demonstrated the effectiveness of traditional and marathon groups in improving classroom behavior for low-performing middle-grade students (Campbell & Myrick, 1990). Yet another study showed that group counseling reduced the number of problems of elementary school children and improved their achievement (Schechtman, 1993). A group guidance and group counseling intervention improved the grade point averages of adolescents (Schnedeker, 1991).

Various models of group work can be useful for bettering school performance. An early study of Adlerian group therapy with adolescent girls (ages 13 to 17) showed an increase in grade point averages (Thoma, 1964). Behavioral group approaches have been useful in working with urban second- to sixth-grade students at risk for dropping out of school (Charney, 1993). Contingency contracting combined with group counseling reduced truancy in mildly handicapped middle school children (Hess, Rosenberg, & Levy, 1990). Peer counseling and achievement motivation groups resulted in improved attendance in middle school youngsters (Shorey, 1981).

A few school performance studies have been less encouraging. For instance, one early study showed little effect of group work on the self-concept, academic performance, and reading level of adolescents in high school (Armstrong, 1978). Another study showed fairly negative results of group work with low-achieving high school students (Catterall, 1987).

The body of evaluation research just cited shows that group work effectively can help members cope with divorce and improve their peer relationships, mental health, and school performance. Considerable progress has been made in determining which kinds of group work are effective to what degree with which children and adolescents with which problems in which schools and communities and ultimately, from a theoretical and research perspective, why. Further research will help answer such a multifaceted question to an even greater extent than is available through current knowledge.

THE FUTURE OF GROUP WORK

The strengths of group work with children and adolescents include providing a developmentally appropriate and naturalistic arena for socialization, social support, and social exchange. Group work has the capacity to provide individualization; it indirectly influences and is related to the family system and is linked to school and community systems.

Group work provides a context that tends to be supportive to the cultural identity of minority children and adolescents. Ashby, Gilchrist, and Miramontez (1987) used group work to promote values clarification, identification with American Indian ways, and skill building in communication, problem solving, and emotional expression for sexually abused adolescents. Still, delivering services that are ethnically and culturally sensitive can be further emphasized. Culturally sensitive practice issues include building rapport with children whose family members have experienced violence, contracting with children who have limited language skills and authority (Congress & Lynn, 1994). Such an approach has demonstrated value. For instance, group work has been shown to promote the capacity of immigrant Hispanic adolescents for competence and mastery over their new environment (Lopez, 1991).

More services for adolescents can be aimed at improving intergroup relations. For example, parents and teachers were concerned about the levels of aggression and violence in a large urban high school. A group leader who practiced in the school called a meeting in which conflictual relationships between two ethnic-racial groups was identified as one of the problems. After consultation and discussions with many parties, the leader decided to work separately within each ethnic-racial group to see whether each had the ability to constructively resolve conflict.

Then, the leader carefully composed a mixed group consisting of adolescents from the two antagonistic groups. Whereas this was perceived by a consultant to be risky because of the potential for the escalation of animosity, the strategy promoted tolerance of each other's presence and furthered the understanding of each other's point of view.

Finally, more efforts should be made to design and deliver preventive and interventive group work for improving the health and well-being of adolescents, which is challenged by severe problems, including HIV infection and AIDS, pregnancy, smoking, alcoholism and other drug abuse, and violent and antisocial behavior (Wiener, Spencer, Davidson, & Fair, 1993). Many such services are likely to be either based in or linked to school systems (Carlson, Paavola, & Talley, 1995).

CONCLUSION

The first part of this book provides the basis for understanding and conducting group work in school and community systems. The focus of this work is on practice with members who, while encountering life stressors, are functioning well enough in society so that they are not institutionalized. Group work, as presented here, has a cognitive base and emphasizes problem solving, which is broadly considered to include activities carried out by members and leaders. Problem solving is creative and systematic. Whereas problem solving here emphasizes interpersonal relations (see Chapter 7), in some instances impersonal aspects also are important (see Chapter 9).

The applications of group work vary to some extent, depending on whether the members are children or are adolescents (see Chapter 3). Group work involves a focus on a specific problem. Part II displays the application of a problem-solving model of group work with children and adolescents with specific variations depending on which problem is the subject of focus. The next part of the book considers the types of problems of children and adolescents for which group work is applied, including parental divorce (Chapter 6), peer relationships and social competence (Chapter 7), mental health and substance abuse (Chapter 8), and school performance (Chapter 9).

PART II

APPLICATIONS OF GROUP WORK

Chapter 6

PARENTAL DIVORCE

DIVORCE AS A SOCIAL PROBLEM

Family difficulties, including marital separation and divorce, affect the social, emotional, and psychological functioning of school-age children. Group work with children and adolescents that addresses family problems has evolved to emphasize the impact of divorce. This chapter will examine the use of group work with youngsters who are affected by parental divorce, a pervasive social problem.

Some estimates indicate that half of all children will be affected by divorce (Cordell & Bergman-Meador, 1991). Each year more than one million children experience parental divorce (National Center for Health Statistics, 1990). Many couples divorce when their children are of school age (Glassman & Reid, 1985). In some schools, children of divorce form the majority of students (Pines, 1982).

The perceptions of the child and relevant others influence the emotional impact of the divorce experience. Children of divorce usually feel abandoned, anxious, depressed, isolated, and rejected (Hetherington, 1979). Children's emotional concerns include fearing that the custodial parent will leave, fearing that if they express anger to the noncustodial parent that parent will decide not to see them again, wishing not to be punished for being angry with the parent, and being more upset at the anger of the stepparent than of the parent (Farmer & Galaris, 1993). Early elementary-school-age children of divorce often feel very sad and wish their parents would get back together. Frequently, such children are confused about the divorce and what it means for their own relationships to people in the family. They may blame themselves for the divorce. They have the emotional issues of separation when they leave the custodial parent and are concerned about visiting the noncustodial parent. Positive feelings they may experience for stepparents and eventually their parents' partners stir up conflicts of loyalty for them.

In addition to emotional difficulties, many children of divorce tend to lag behind their peers in academic achievement, popularity, and adjustment to school (Pasternack & Peres, 1990). The impact of divorce varies with the gender and age of the youngsters (Wallerstein & Kelly, 1976). For instance, 9- and 10-year-old children tend to be particularly vulnerable to disruption in school performance (Kanoy & Cunningham, 1984).

Whereas divorce is currently less stigmatized than was previously the case (Lesowitz, Kalter, Pickar, Chethik, & Schaefer, 1987), it remains a difficult experience for children and adolescents. They frequently demonstrate problematic emotional reactions and mental health difficulties, which sometimes persist a decade after the divorce (Cebollero, Cruise, & Stollak, 1987). Children of divorce have more school attendance difficulties and higher dropout rates, more difficulties in social interaction, classroom conduct that interferes with performance and that requires extra attention by the teacher, and have a greater number of learning disorders than other children (Guidubaldi, Cleminshaw, Perry, & McLaughlin, 1983). Children of divorce have higher rates of externalizing problems, including acting out, aggression, and conduct disorder (Forehand, Thomas, Wierson, Brody, & Fauber, 1990) and internalizing problems, including anxiety, depression, and withdrawal (Hoyt, Cowen, Pedro-Carroll, & Alpert-Gillis, 1990) than children from intact families. Children or adolescents with observable mental health problems prior to divorce have the potential to experience an exacerbation of such problems on learning of the impending separation and divorce, witnessing the departure or absence of a parent, and living with the reality of a significant change in the family structure.

Youngsters who are in conflicted families often find it difficult to concentrate on their studies (Borrine, Handal, Brown, & Searight, 1991). Indeed, interpersonal conflict appears to be the principal explanation for the association between divorce and ensuing problems of adolescents (Fauber, Long, & McCombs, 1988). Children's degree of comfort with the separation and divorce process is inversely related to the level of acrimonious parental interaction (Farmer & Galaris, 1993). Children and adolescents who are distracted from learning in school, because of their cognitive and emotional responses to family events, are less likely to achieve satisfactorily than other youngsters. In the first year following divorce, school work tends to be impaired in two out of three children (Kelly & Wallerstein, 1979). Furthermore, family conflict also is related to conflict at school. Children of divorce are more likely than other children to be engaged in conflict in school systems (Evans & Neel, 1980). A continuity of stress exists in predivorce situations, during divorce, and postdivorce. The effects of divorce may even outlast those of the death of a family member (Graver, 1987). The stressors include hostility between parents, the distress of the custodial parent, a change and loss in relationship with the noncustodial parent, parent dating, remarriage, downward economic mobility, and change in residence (Kalter & Schreier, 1994).

PURPOSE OF GROUP WORK

Changes in the structure and dynamics of the family, along with a sense of victimization and suffering that many youngsters in divorcing families experience, are subject to remediation through group work. Children often feel freer to express themselves in groups than they do in individual or family therapies (Schreier & Kalter, 1990).

Groups for children who are experiencing parental separation or divorce provide members with the chance to recognize and share their experiences with peers (Williams, 1984). Indeed, many children become comfortable discussing upsetting events in groups with children who have experienced similar events. The presence of youngsters encountering, sharing, and understanding related problems often mitigates against a sense of isolation, produces a sense of camaraderie, and improves morale. Youngsters see that their peers are struggling with similar problems and feelings.

The overall purpose of the group work is to improve the social adjustment of youngsters whose parents have divorced. It has the advantage of increasing members' ease about family issues that might interfere with their concentration, attention, and learning.

Children's adjustment to parental divorce is facilitated through the provision of social support, which buffers them from stressful family situations (Kurdek, 1988). The benefits of being part of a social group are particularly useful for those who are part of a separated or divorced family. A supportive group normalizes the phenomenon of divorce for the children who are affected by it (Mervis, 1989).

Often, group work with young children focuses on their attaining a realistic appraisal of family events culminating in divorce (Epstein, Borduin, & Wexler, 1985). Young children are often able to attain relief about their own situation and acquire compassion and understanding of youngsters who experience similar situations. Group work is meant to overcome the sense of isolation that children encounter with the experience of parental divorce. An objective is to help members attain greater happiness and to learn to express their emotional reactions to divorce, including anger, in a constructive manner. An objective of group work with adolescents is for them to recognize and reduce the influence of conflictual patterns of family dynamics so that they will be less likely to replicate such patterns.

Owing to the prevalence of divorce, group work with children of divorce has become a widespread phenomenon in school and community systems (Tedder et al., 1987). Most group work programs for divorce are for elementary-school-age children and are provided in schools (Cordell & Bergman-Meador, 1991). Whereas some groups for children of divorce are conducted in mental health centers, estimates are that at least 20 times as many are conducted in schools (Grych & Fincham, 1992).

Schools are appropriate places for many reasons for the use of group work to help children of divorce (Burnett & Newcomer, 1990). Many children of divorce are present in schools. In schools, group work is a time-efficient means of addressing the social and emotional concerns of individual youngsters. Public schools are appropriate sites for reaching children whose families might otherwise be unable to pay for service (Cowen et al., 1989). Children already spend a large portion of their day in schools and they have ready access to services provided in the school (Mervis, 1989). Providing group work to children of divorce in the school during the course of their regular days promotes a normalization of the divorce experience (Schreier & Kalter, 1990). Schools provide a structure and continuity that is useful to children who are in the midst of major family transitions, such as divorce (Graver, 1987). In school systems, peers are readily available to provide the validation and support that is crucial for older children and adolescents (Mervis, 1989). Schools are appropriate places for addressing problems of divorce, which interfere with children's learning. The social, emotional, and academic problems that tend to ensue with divorce are observed by teachers who are challenged with working with such children (Mervis, 1989). Group work programs in schools can become self-perpetuating as they become known to and accepted by children, their families, and school staff at the school and as group leaders continue to work in the schools.

School-based groups for children of divorce meet multiple purposes (Pfeifer & Abrams, 1984). The organization of groups signifies that children are facing challenges in adapting to stressful events. The groups provide clarification and information about divorce and family life. They provide an opportunity to come to terms with the past, deal with the present, and sense what the future holds. They also provide opportunities for the leaders to discover which children may require more intensive help.

Many group work programs for children of divorce have specific goals (Prokop, 1990). One goal is to foster a supportive environment. A second goal is to facilitate the identification and expression of divorce-related feelings. Given that many children and adolescents experience confusion over parental divorce, including reasons for the divorce and warning about the divorce (Neugebauer, 1989), a third goal is to promote understanding of divorce-related concepts and clarify divorce-related misconceptions. A fourth goal is to teach problem-solving skills. A fifth goal is to enhance positive perceptions of self and family.

Schreier and Kalter (1990) identified a similar set of goals for groups to help children of divorce. One goal is using information and peer support to provide a normalization of the experience of divorce. A second goal is to clarify divorce-related concerns. A third goal is to rework emotionally difficult aspects of the divorce. A fourth goal is to help the youngsters cope with the divorce as a stressful experience. A fifth goal is to promote greater parental support and involvement with their children through communication of the latter's responses to the divorce.

PROBLEM RECOGNITION
AND SOLUTION

The recognition of family problems prior to, during, or consequent to divorce is facilitated by communication among family, school, and community systems. Changes in children's family life are noted on parental information forms at school registration. Intense reactions of children to divorce are readily observed by leaders, who may become aware of the family changes that have taken place. The "warning signs" of elementary and middle school children of divorce include "moodiness, temper tantrums, crying spells, daydreaming, physical aggression, a decrease in academic performance and the ability to concentrate, lethargic work habits, physical complaints, an increased need for assurance, and increased acting out" (Prokop, 1990, p. 72). Through pregroup interviews with youngsters and family members and the use of instruments (Brown, Haas, & Portes, 1991; Pedro-Carroll et al., 1989), assessment of the functioning of the youngsters within the divorce situation, involving knowledge of circumstances, is obtained.

In many school and community systems a desire exists to help youngsters whose parents have divorced. Nevertheless, in some communities and schools, divorce remains a sensitive topic. The sanction and authorization for group work is dependent on the conceptualization of the problem and the values of the program being offered.

Once the problems attendant to divorce are recognized, problem solving begins. Interpersonal conflict is resolved through compromise, win or lose approaches, and problem solving (Coffman, 1988). In group work, members with family problems recognize and identify the family component and context of their difficulties. Problematic aspects are subject to remediation and destigmatization.

Timing influences the type of group that is used. Group work often follows parental divorce, the breaking point in a family in which major conflict, disequilibrium, and crisis occur (Homes & Rahe, 1967). Indeed, much group work incorporates principles of crisis intervention to help members (Lesowitz et al., 1987). Whereas the period immediately following divorce is often the focus of attention, the waves of difficulty in succeeding years, particularly for young children, are also worthy of attention.

In the Divorce Adjustment Project (DAP), a preventive program for children of divorce, Stolberg and Mahler (1989) developed a problem-solving approach in the Children's Support Group (CSG). Six cognitive steps are used. The first step is "What's the Problem?" With the use of a cartoon, members are taught to ask themselves to identify the problem. The second step is "What Are My Choices?" They are instructed to list all possible solutions to the problem that they have identified. The third step is "If I Do _____, Then _____ Might Happen." Members learn to evaluate each possible solution in regard to the potential consequences of implementation. The fourth step is "Make A Choice." They learn to choose from among the possible solutions. The fifth step is "Was That A Good Choice?" Members evaluate the effectiveness of the choice in terms of its consequences. The sixth step is "Pat Yourself on the Back— Or—Try Again." They learn to say good things to themselves about their problem-solving performance or to recognize lack of success that necessitates further action.

PLANNING AND COMPOSITION

Planning for group work with children of divorce involves a consideration of their emotional vulnerabilities. Given that coping skills of children are a major factor in the adjustment of children to divorce (Brown et al., 1991), leaders plan activities to bolster the coping capacities of members in dealing with stressors and in solving problems. In schools, leaders prepare reminders for sessions that they send to the teachers (Hoffman, 1984). Leaders also prepare evaluation forms, which are completed by members at the end of each session. Such forms provide members with the opportunity to provide the leaders with feedback and to indicate topics that they wish to address.

Several considerations exist in selecting members, including that their parents are separated or divorced (Sonnenshein-Schneider & Baird, 1980). For youngsters who are doing well, group work may provide peer support, promote self-esteem, bolster extant coping styles, and verify the reality and commonality of their experiences with parental divorce. For youngsters who are struggling with the many issues surrounding divorce, group work may help them identify and cope with stressors, including irregular patterns of visiting with the noncustodial parent, conflict and aggression between parents, and remarriage of one or both parents. The group is likely to include those for whom it is their sole professional means of help as well as some members who are receiving additional professional help, such as individual counseling or psychotherapy.

In schools and communities that have many children with family problems, finding sufficient numbers of children or adolescents who will interact, work well together, and benefit from participation is feasible. Indeed, in schools and communities that have a large population of youngsters who experience parental divorce, it is often feasible for leaders to include youngsters who have experienced divorce at the same age and in the same grade. In addition to children whose parents have recently divorced, youngsters whose parents have divorced many years ago also are able to benefit from membership (Garvin, Leber, & Kalter, 1991).

At times children wish to be in same-sex groups as a way of enhancing confidentiality, understanding, and comfort, as with third- through fifth-grade children in school groups (Cole & Kammer, 1984). Nevertheless, having groups composed of both girls and boys has been recommended (Strauss & McGann, 1987). Ideally, mixed-sex groups should be composed of approximately equal numbers of girls and boys (Kalter & Schreier, 1994).

It is preferable to have separate groups for young children (ages 6 to 9) and older children (ages 9 to 12) (Strauss & McGann, 1987). Working with younger children involves spending additional time clarifying the concepts of divorce, distinguishing between fantasy and reality in role playing, and using such materials as drawing, which allows youngsters to express themselves and to deal with intense emotions of divorce that are brought up by activities. In comparison with younger children, older children usually tend to be more verbal and articulate. Older children more quickly benefit from discussions and sharing of feelings and experiences related to divorce, more readily understand what is happening in their families in regard to causes and events, and are more likely to use information to deal with difficulties. Furthermore, older children are sensitive to issues of confidentiality and are more interested that material that is discussed not be shared directly with parents.

In comparison with the large numbers of divorce groups for children, relatively few divorce groups are available for adolescents. Nevertheless, some leaders have organized adolescent groups with sessions dealing with health, emotions, learning, personal relationships, image, desire to know correct information, and guidance of actions and consequences (Crosbie-Burnett & Newcomer, 1990).

Some divorce groups have as many as 10 members (Grych & Fincham, 1992). Nevertheless, optimal size ranges between four and seven members for early elementary-school-age groups (grades one to three) and between four and eight members for later elementary-school-age groups (grades four to six) (Schreier & Kalter, 1990). Between five and nine members also have been recommended for groups of children ages 6 through 12, with 2- to 4-year age spans represented (Epstein et al., 1985). Nevertheless, to maximize cohesion it is argued that early elementary-school-age groups should be composed of four to seven youngsters who are within one grade and later elementary-school-age groups should be composed of five to eight youngsters who are within two grades (Kalter & Schreier, 1994).

It is useful to have children from the same grade as it provides them with a sense of similarity. Nevertheless, for older children and adolescents a one-grade difference can be workable. Furthermore, members who are at different stages of the divorce process help one another set realistic expectations and provide support. The group may include members who are experiencing recent parental separation, members who are dealing with relocation, and members who are dealing with

some step along the way of parental dating, remarriage, and the formation of stepfamilies. Nevertheless, for the group to coalesce, it should
be so constituted that all members have someone else in it who has
experienced the same aspect of divorce (Sonnenshein-Schneider &
Baird, 1980).

LEADERSHIP AND ACTIVITIES

Given the emotional concerns of children of divorce, it is important
that as parental figures adult leaders project an accepting and at times
nurturing stance to the members. Active leadership promotes participation in discussion and structured activities to promote empathy, insight,
and shared understanding of family relationships. For members who
have witnessed destructive parental conflict, coleadership often is beneficial in displaying constructive adult interaction (Farmer & Galaris,
1993). Although using female and male coleaders appears best in most
group work with children of divorce (Kalter, Schaefer, Lesowitz,
Alpern, & Pickar, 1988), female coleaders have been shown to be useful
with adolescent girls (Kostoulas, Berkovitz, & Arima, 1991).

Often, process, such as addressing conflicts in daily living, is given
precedence by the leaders over the accomplishment of projects, such as
audiovisual production (Bowker, 1982). The process inevitably relates
to the actual experience of the members. Whereas general situations
often are presented as are experiences of hypothetical youngsters, the
members themselves are likely to bring up their own actual experiences
with divorce.

Leaders use creative activities for expressing and diffusing emotions
brought up by family difficulties. Drawing, puppet shows, role playing,
storytelling, and games appeal to the senses of young children and
provide them with the opportunity to express themselves in a comfortable, spontaneous, and enjoyable manner (Cebollero et al., 1987).
Drawings are means of communication that are used by young children
to express the significant experiences of divorce, to symbolically represent family relationships, and to describe the home situation
(Oppawsky, 1991). They are particularly useful for young children and
some boys of school age who are uncomfortable or unable to directly

talk about their feelings (Cordell & Bergman-Meador, 1991). Drawings express the emotions of children during divorce, including open protest against parents, and are a socially accepted way to express anger, which is a frequent emotional reaction of children to divorce. Leaders can ask children of divorce to draw one picture of their family and another picture of the noncustodial or absent parent (Sonnenshein-Schneider & Baird, 1980).

Affective education techniques also are sometimes used to help children become aware of their feelings that are caused by divorce (Effron, 1980). Leaders teach children to identify divorce-related feelings and associate them with particular situations and events.

Reading and writing activities are often useful for elementary school age children of divorce (Cole & Kammer, 1984). Some children write and read poems about divorce-related themes. Topics for creative writing projects that have been suggested by elementary school children (Effron, 1980) include

> being caught in a custody fight and understanding the functioning of family relations court, anticipating a visit by your father after you haven't seen him for almost a year, how to react when an older sibling moves out of the house, and the extra responsibilities of living in a one-parent home. (p. 311)

The members create and produce a newspaper providing news and information about divorce (Lesowitz et al., 1987). Children and adolescents are able to participate in video projects.

Sometimes television shows are produced that deal with divorce-related themes. Young children, ages 5 to 11, are able to write and appear in plays that they produce for video (Mervis, 1989). Often, they are more comfortable than older children with plays that contain material relating to problems of alcoholism, domestic violence, suicide, and mental health.

Another activity is keeping journals. Journals allow children to express private thoughts and feelings about divorce. The journals are written in a free-form style based on themes that are presented in a particular session. For example, "I wish I could tell my dad. . . . " Bibliotherapy is related to keeping journals. Children are given a book to read, such as *The Boys and Girls Books About Divorce* (Gardner,

1970). The members write in their journals about how such a book, and the feelings described, are applicable to their own situations.

Another idea for writing pertains to children of divorce who turn into latchkey kids, who are often in the position of spending considerable time alone at home. They can develop written plans for how to take care of and cope by themselves.

Children and adolescents readily engage in role playing and discussion sequences. Role playing is useful in developing communication and interaction skills and in revealing how children react to conflict between parents (Effron, 1980).

Through role playing, members recognize that others encounter similar problems. They also learn to face the reality of their own life situations. Members learn active means of coping with difficult situations that they confront in their changed living situations and are often able to develop creative solutions to problems that the divorce situation presents. The members list problems created by divorce, which usually relate to fighting, drinking, money, and lack of love between parents, rank them, and enact the problems in the role play (Cutsinger & Glick, 1983). Leaders participate in role playing by portraying arguments between parents that precede divorce (Kalter et al., 1984).

A component of brainstorming, which is useful in conjunction with role playing, readily can be used as a means of helping members devise possible solutions to the problems they encounter in divorce situations (Sonnenshein-Schneider & Baird, 1980). The members think of as many problems as they can that were created by the divorce and then rank them in importance. Brief role plays follow, which involve enacting the problem situations.

Many groups meet once a week for 45 or 50 minutes and are short-term, lasting up to about 12 weeks (Cutsinger & Glick, 1983). Groups for younger children often meet for more sessions, for example, 10 sessions, than group for older children, for example, eight sessions (Kalter & Schreier, 1994).

The structure of groups is apparent in topics that are assigned for particular sessions. For instance, the sessions of one group consisted of (a) I'm not so different, which countered feelings of isolation; (b) balancing, which restored equilibrium despite the changes that accompany divorce; (c) loyalty, which helped members deal with conflicts stemming from being pulled in different directions toward parents who were no longer together; (d) sharing, which promoted discussions of feelings; (e) other people, which served youngsters in dealing with new people in the home; and (f) summary session, which reviewed concepts from preceding sessions (Admunson-Beckmann & Lucas, 1989).

In an elementary-school-age children's group (Anderson et al., 1984), the first session was used to establish goals and rules and to play get-acquainted games. In the second session, the members practiced self-disclosure through writing information about themselves on paper. In the third session, the leaders showed a film about divorce, which served as a stimulus for a discussion they conducted about divorce. In the fourth session, the members drew four sets of pictures: good times spent with family, an event that made the family feel sad, something you do to make the family feel happy, and how you feel about your parents' divorce. In the fifth session, the leaders conducted a brainstorming and role-playing session about divorce-related problems. In the sixth session, the members discussed topics related to difficulties and improvements following divorce. In the seventh session, the members drew portraits of themselves and of family members and listed good things about each person represented in the drawings. In the eighth session, members took turns occupying a seat and receiving compliments, which was followed by a discussion by all the members.

In an early version of the Children of Divorce Intervention Program (CODIP) for youngsters in the fourth through sixth grades, sessions 1 to 3 formed the affective component, sessions 4 to 6 comprised the cognitive and problem-solving skill-building component, sessions 7 to 9 emphasized anger expression and control, and session 10 focused on evaluation and dealing with feelings at the ending (Pedro-Carroll & Cowen, 1985).

In a more recent version of the CODIP program for elementary-school-aged children (Pedro-Carroll et al., 1992), the first four sessions focus on emotional concerns. In session 1, the leaders conduct acquaintanceship exercises, a game in which feelings are drawn from a grab bag, and have the members come up with a name and symbol to encourage cohesiveness. In session 2, the leaders use books and discussions to encourage greater awareness and acceptance of family structures that differ from those of the nuclear family. In session 3, the leaders show films to stimulate discussion of divorce. In session 4, the leaders use creative activities, including writing, drawing, poetry, humor, and making a newsletter to help members express their frustrations and develop cohesiveness.

Sessions 5 to 11 of the CODIP program for elementary-school-age children explicitly focus on the development of coping skills and resilience in the face of major stressors. Sessions 5 and 6 are devoted to the acquisition of interpersonal-cognitive problem-solving skills applied to divorce issues. In session 7, the leaders use a red light-green light game to help members learn to identify which problem situations are within their control. Session 8 employs the format of a television panel discussion of experts to handle questions about divorce from the audience. The leaders help members develop their mastery and sense of competence in knowing how to handle difficult situations that they often encounter in their daily lives. In sessions 9 to 11, the leaders use games, such as stop and think, and instant replay, to help members develop control over anger engendered by the divorce and improve their communication skills.

In sessions 12 and 13, the leaders aim to improve members' self-esteem. The members play a "kids are special people" board game. Feedback and discussions of the contributions and strengths of each member are designed to promote self-esteem. The leaders give each member a caring card, which records positive statements from other members, to take home. The leaders conduct a discussion of how things have improved in members' homes following the divorce. The leaders also facilitate discussions about termination, which is addressed in terms of graduation.

In session 14, the final meeting, the leaders hold a discussion of the entire group experience as well as feelings around termination. The leaders present ideas about obtaining support through friendships. The group shares certificates of graduation and photographs.

AN EXAMPLE: THE FAMILY WINNERS

At a small, urban elementary school on the outskirts of a heterogenous neighborhood, the family concerns of pupils caught the attention of B. J., a social worker who provided social services at several schools in the city. Through discussions she held with teachers at the school, B. J. discovered that such problems were widely manifested in and around the school.

One teacher told B. J. about Shelly, a second-grade student whose parents had divorced more than a year ago. Shelly had bedrooms in two houses, divided her time between them, and was uncertain which house was her home. Shelly's teacher was unable to comprehend the youngster's confusion at having two homes. When the teacher asked Shelly to describe her homes, the girl pointed out the differences in the wallpaper pattern and mentioned that in her father's home there was a dog she liked. Ultimately, Shelly was referred for a mental health evaluation.

Another teacher told B. J. of a youngster who did not know what he should call his stepparent. At a wedding they attended, the boy and his new stepfather did not know how to address one another when they were introduced to a distant cousin.

A third-grade teacher told B. J. about April, a child who was concerned about the stability of her newly reconstituted family. April had noticed that her mother had switched the chair she customarily sat in at the dinner table, just as she did before April's father had left the family.

Several teachers confided to B. J. that pupils' family issues interfered with teaching processes in their classrooms and distracted the children from learning. One teacher found Alexia, a third-grade student, staring out of the classroom window instead of doing a subtraction exercise. When she asked Alexia what she was thinking about, the girl said it was her mom and she began to cry.

From discussions that she held with the teachers, pupil-personnel-service staff, and administrators, B. J. concluded that many of the children at the school were in changing families and were not coping well with the changes. She considered a number of treatment modalities for providing services to children. Nevertheless, when she thought of what level of intervention the pupils would like and what intervention was likely to be effective, she decided on group work for children of divorce. Most of the teachers whom B. J. polled seemed interested in such a group and some even volunteered to colead it!

To discuss the group, which would be the first of its kind to be held in the school, B. J. held an informational meeting for teachers and staff.

Several teachers and the assistant principal showed up at the meeting
and expressed their support. After a review of the proposed group and
a discussion with the assistant principal, the principal gave her consent
for the school-based program to be implemented at the beginning of the
next school year.

The group was planned by B. J. during the final weeks of the spring
semester. Although she was aware of family difficulties among the
younger elementary school children, she felt that she would be most
effective with some of the older children.

At the beginning of the next school year, B. J. learned that many
fourth-grade children were having difficulties associated with conflictual home settings. She requested and, to her surprise, received the
names of children who appeared to the fourth-grade teachers to be
adversely affected by parental divorce. On scanning the lists, she recognized most of the names, although she was astonished to see a few
names of children whose families were in turmoil. After talking with
the teachers, B. J. decided to observe fourth-grade classrooms and to
pay special attention to those few children whom she did not know very
well. Her observations were informal and informative. She felt that she
knew the children better by observing them in the classroom.

Later, B. J. interviewed 14 children for the group for children of
divorce. Two seemed unsuitable for the group: one was immature and
the other was antisocial. Ultimately, she received written consent from
the parents of seven children who gave their assent for participating in
the group. Four boys and three girls formed the group.

Although the teachers previously had expressed an interest in colead-
ing the group, extra administrative assignments prevented them from
carrying out such plans. The group was led by B. J. on her own.

She organized a 6-week program with two sessions per week. The
first week of the group was devoted to introductions and an orientation
of members to the purpose of the group, which, as she saw it, was to
help the members cope with changes in their families so as to improve
their adjustment at school. Most of the members were already well
acquainted with one another. The members and B. J. planned the activities and sessions. The members listened attentively to B. J.'s ideas, and
she responded to their questions, for example, "Can we tell our parents
about this class?" They considered a number of names for the group,

including "The Family Finders" and "The Family Detectives." Ultimately, they decided on "The Family Winners."

In the second week of the group work program, the members discussed school friends as potential and actual sources of support, which helped buffer the stressors they experienced at home. The leader, B. J., decided to form friendship couples so that active support could be exchanged in the group. She was also interested in extending the social circle outside the group to partially compensate for members' losses experienced in the family. As a means of assessment, each child drew pictures of everyone they knew in relation to how close they were to them.

She also assessed the participation of family members at school events. Some of the members reported that they had been upset about not having both parents attend school functions. Although the members recognized that the reason for the absence of a parent was the conflict between the parents, it still felt to many members as if both parents did not love them.

In the third week of the group, B. J. led a discussion of changes in the membership of families through events, such as birth, adoption, death, and divorce. Members cut out pictures from magazines devoted to stages of the family life cycle, glued them in workbooks, and spontaneously discussed what changes had occurred in their own families.

The members were at various stages of the divorce process. Those members whose parents were in the midst of a divorce tended to listen avidly to the stories of those members whose parents had divorced some time earlier. One member recounted how when she was 9 years old she was abruptly told one morning by her mother that her parents were divorcing. "But what will happen to me?" Sheila remembered she cried as she ran out of the house. She laughed as she described how it took her mother more than an hour to find her.

In the fourth week of the group, the members discussed the relationship between family life and school performance, a topic that appeared to make many of them anxious. Recognizing the members' discomfort, the leader showed the children how to relax. The members identified athletic, musical, and social activities that they could conduct outside of the group.

The members recounted scenarios that tended to interfere with how they did in school. When one child reported that her parents' screaming at each other made it difficult for her to concentrate, several others nodded their heads knowingly. The members thought of alternate sites for studying, such as their friends' homes. Indeed, the members were happy to get out of their own tumultuous homes. To B. J. it seemed like a respite for them.

The group used a problem-solving approach to help a member who indicated that her father no longer was available to help her with her math homework. Fran was starting to get low grades in math and, much to the leader's satisfaction, she turned to the group for assistance. The members thought of people Fran could talk to at school, including themselves, and the leader gave Fran a phone number of an assistance line staffed by teachers.

In the fifth week, B. J. decided to focus on communication between the members' homes and their more stable school. A fourth-grade teacher who supervised the school grounds told B. J. of the parents of one of the members who neglected to pick him up from the after-school program. When the teacher called home, the boy's mother, who had recently remarried, was surprised at the call. In a surprising move, a member of the pupil personnel team had contacted the local child welfare service, which warned the boy's mother of the consequences of neglect.

Earlier, B. J. had sent home notes to the parents and had received some replies. With permission she read some of the notes aloud and they were discussed in the group.

The group was nearing completion. During the sixth week the members reviewed coping strategies. Members thought of problem-solving methods they had learned in the group. Many members were uncertain about their families' future. Plans were made for a reunion the following school year. Finally, the members evaluated the group program by completing a questionnaire. In reviewing the results of the questionnaires the members had completed, as well as considering the results of postgroup interviews that she conducted with the members, B. J. concluded that the members appeared to have benefited from emotion-based and practical strategies for coping with family conflict and parental divorce. Members had learned to find support within and outside the group and were able to ventilate their feelings. Moreover, they had developed their skills in relaxation methods, conflict mediation, decision making, and problem solving.

To share her experiences with the group for children of divorce, B. J. then held a meeting with the teachers and staff of the elementary school. Attendees expressed an interest in continuing the program the following year. A separate program was held for parents of the children who had participated in the group. The few parents who came expressed their support for the group as well. The parents who did not come to the meeting were called by B. J., to gather their views.

CONCLUSION

As the culmination of family conflict, divorce affects youngsters in many ways and often significantly hampers their social and academic performance. Group work with children and adolescents is a useful means of helping members cope with family changes and the stressors that accompany divorce.

Often, the timing and emphasis of group work is interventive and occurs after parental divorce, rather than being preventive and occurring before divorce. Nevertheless, some group work reflects a combination of prevention and intervention strategies designed to help members cope with current difficulties and forestall problems that are likely to occur later on in their lives.

Whereas the present chapter has been concerned with the consequences of disruptions in members family relationships, the following chapter is devoted to their peer social relationships.

Chapter 7

PEER RELATIONSHIPS AND SOCIAL COMPETENCE

PEER RELATIONSHIPS AND SOCIAL COMPETENCE AS A SOCIAL PROBLEM

Many persons, including group leaders, tend to be concerned about the development of social competence of children and adolescents. Such concerns range from the manners of children to the lack of stability in marital and family systems. Indeed, as seen in the previous chapter, the effects of divorce tend to be considerable in terms of the changes in socialization, relationships, and availability of parental role models experienced by children. This chapter will describe the concept of social competence, discuss problems of children and adolescents who possess low levels of social competence, and indicate how leaders address such problems through group work.

As children and adolescents mature they usually develop their understanding of feelings, their capacity to display and demonstrate emotions, and their ability to form and maintain social relationships. The development of such understanding and abilities are the focus of social competence group work.

Social competence is necessary for the achievement of the academic goals that are the traditional aims of education as well as furthering friendships and social relationships among youngsters that are vital to their interpersonal development.

Socially competent children and adolescents act to reach their goals within reciprocal dyadic relationships. Often, the appropriateness of social goal-seeking activity is considered in group work. Children and adolescents vary in regard to their levels of social competence. Adequate levels of social competence are associated with sound interpersonal relationships, social adjustment, and mental health. Children and adolescents with adequate peer relationships are more likely to maximize the social aspects of achievement, school performance, and ultimately occupational performance than those with inadequate peer relationships (see Chapter 9).

Some youngsters have high competence levels, as seen in their skillfulness in social interactions, their ability to get along well with others, their popularity, and their friendships. Such youngsters tend to overtly demonstrate or perform social skills in social situations that, for instance, encompass establishing eye contact, greeting a newcomer, and establishing a friendship. In group work, such youngsters may serve as models for youngsters who possess low levels of social competence and have marginal personal relationships.

The lack of sufficient levels of social competence has come to be regarded as a significant handicap for many children and adolescents. Social skills difficulties in children and adolescents are related to social avoidance, stemming from anxiety, lack of motivation due to depression, or a combination of the above factors (Kendall, Kortlander, Chansky, & Brady, 1992; Stark, Rouse, & Livingston, 1991). Nonanxious (confident and relaxed) children are more popular than anxious children (Miller & Gentry, 1980). Social competence group work, consisting in part of social skills training that includes assertiveness, mitigates against anxiety.

The consequences of inadequate social and emotional development and functioning and low levels of social competence of children and adolescents tend to persist into the adult years. Children and adolescents who are socially isolated are more likely to drop out of school, develop mental disorders, be identified as juvenile delinquents, and obtain bad conduct military discharges (Cowen, Pederson, Babigian, Izzo, & Trost, 1973; Kohlberg, LaCrosse, & Ricks, 1972; Kohn & Claussen, 1955; Roff, 1961; Roff, Sells, & Golden, 1972; Ullmann, 1957; Watt, 1979). Many such youngsters should be members of social competence groups.

Low levels of social competence are both a reflection of and a contributor to troubled family relationships. Peer relationships develop out of parent-child relations (Rubin & Pepler, 1980). The difficulties in social interaction of many children and adolescents reflect the stressors experienced by troubled families. Furthermore, children and adolescents with social competence difficulties limit family members and may engender family difficulties. For instance, Jo was a girl who had few friends and whose difficulties in social interaction were apparent in her family. She stayed aloof from members of her family, who expended considerable effort in looking after her. When her problems were recognized she was referred to a community-based social competence group.

The social relationships of children and adolescents are related to their self-concept and sociometric status. High sociometric status is equated with popularity and low status is equated with rejection (Hepler & Rose, 1988). Children who are popular tend to be chosen by many children. Popularity and friendship are related concepts that encompass a bilateral preference and imply some desirable aspects of youngsters' social actions. In social competence groups, members tend to occupy a range of sociometric statuses.

Outgoingness, social visibility, sociability, and friendliness are directly related to children's sociometric acceptance by peers (Hartup, 1970). Acceptance of others, compliance, and cooperation, which are indicators of social flexibility, are positively correlated to peer popularity (Moore, 1967). Such attitudes and skills are often the focus of social competence group work.

Members who have low levels of social competence and who have difficulties in peer relations include those who are neglected, isolated, and rejected. Members who are neglected receive few sociometric nominations from their peers. Members who are isolated have few social relationships. Members who are rejected tend to be disliked by many of their peers. Furthermore, adolescent members provide different levels of support to peers who are in different sociometric statuses (Munsch & Kinchen, 1995).

Cliques influence child and adolescent development and mediate between individual members and their school and community systems.

Children who are in cliques tend to be somewhat more popular than isolated children. In high school, most peer groups tend to be prosocial. Adolescent members who are in prosocial peer groups tend to obtain social approval. The social adjustment of such adolescents and the benefits to society are likely to be positive. In contrast, adolescent members who participate in and are popular within antisocial high school peer groups are likely to have a range of substance abuse, mental health, and school performance problems that are the focus of group work (Downs & Rose, 1991; Rose & Downs, 1989). Furthermore, such adolescent members are more likely to be negatively labeled and have more negative self-concepts than adolescents in prosocial peer groups.

PURPOSE OF GROUP WORK

A major purpose of group work is to help children and adolescents develop constructive peer relationships. It provides an opportunity for youngsters who are neglected to receive attention, those who are isolated to be more socially involved, and those who are rejected to be accepted. Disabled children and adolescents who experience peer relationship difficulties also often can be helped.

Group work provides the means for youngsters to develop their peer relationships and become more socially competent. It allows for skill development and the generalization of learning to school and community systems. The social competence difficulties that are focused on in group work involve social interactions with peers. The members attempt to find ways to resolve interpersonal problems. Desirable outcomes include actual changes, such as forming new friendships.

The group is an appropriate and useful social context for the prevention and remediation of social competence difficulties. Social competence group work can be offered in a supportive manner to those currently free of noticeable difficulties (primary prevention), those experiencing some difficulties (secondary prevention), and those who are experiencing considerable difficulties (tertiary prevention).

PROBLEM RECOGNITION
AND SOLUTION

Often, the sanction and authorization for the establishment and implementation of group work programs that promote social competence stems from the perception of peer relationship problems and the anticipated ability of group work to provide appropriate socialization experiences for members. Many parents are willing to support group work programs that are designed to enhance their youngsters' capacities for constructive social interaction and conflict resolution.

Children and adolescents who ultimately become group members tend to manifest their social competence problems in school and community systems. Some such youngsters tend to draw attention to themselves by their provocative and disruptive actions that are often defined more in terms of conduct, self-control, and delinquency than social competence. James was invited by several youths to come along with them as they entered and vandalized an abandoned house. Afterward, the youth scattered. Nonetheless, James was questioned by a local patrolman who spotted him in the vicinity. James was warned and let go by the local policeman. Thereafter, James continued to be a lonely and socially isolated preadolescent who could have benefited from social competence group work.

School and community personnel usually are able to detect social competence problems and refer youngsters with such problems for group work. Nonetheless, obstacles exist if staff lack proper training and orientation to identify such problems. The staff at a large urban community center expressed an interest in offering group work programs aimed at improving the social competence of children from the neighborhood who attended programs at the center. Nonetheless, the staff lacked sufficient knowledge to assess the social relationships of children who attended the center to determine membership and form social competence groups. After meetings with the supervisors at the center, the regional training director sent the staff to a course on social competence development. Thereafter, the staff spent more time getting to know the youngsters who participated in the community programs and were better able to assess their social competencies.

At times, poor communication exists within the school or community system relative to the reporting of social competence difficulties. For example, in a school system undergoing restructuring owing to court orders, relatively little attention was paid to the social relationships of the children. Those teachers and social workers who noticed that some children were having difficulty in making friends at school tended to be ignored, as most attention was paid to the efforts of the school to follow court orders.

An additional obstacle occurs if the school or community system is large relative to the number of personnel available to provide social services. Nine thousand students attended one impoverished urban high school. The small pupil personnel staff was overwhelmed with difficulties pertaining to controlling pervasive violence and drug abuse in the school and had little time to attend to issues of social competence.

Finally, the social competence difficulties of shy and unassertive youngsters are less likely to be recognized and assessed than those of disruptive youngsters. In one class consisting of many discourteous preadolescents, the teacher was pleased with Ellen who, in being well-mannered, differed substantially from the others. It was only after Ellen had a personal crisis and made a suicide gesture that it became apparent to school officials and family members that Ellen had significant social competence and mental health difficulties.

One means by which leaders assess the peer relationships and social competence of members is interviewing. Moderate to highly structured interviews are often most useful for assessment purposes.

Self-report measures of social skill and social competence are designed to be completed by the members. They respond to written questions and report how they believe they would interact in social situations.

The teacher's perceptions of members also is vital for assessing social competence. Teacher-completed measures assess social and academic functioning.

Sociometric instruments measure members' social status, including popularity, friendship, social interaction, and peer preference (Alden, Pettigrew, & Skiba, 1970; Blau & Rafferty, 1970; Dunnington, 1957; Singleton & Asher, 1977). Sociometric methods include the roster-and-rating method in which a member answers a sociometric question, such as, "How much do you like to play with this person in school?" for each youngster on a list. In the nomination method members are asked to list a small, given number of their friends.

Role-play tests provide leaders with the opportunity to assess members' abilities to respond to social situations. The Children's Behavioral Roleplay Test was developed for use with 8- to 12-year-old children (Edleson & Rose, 1978). It consists of a dozen situations involving interaction with peers and siblings in school, home, and neighborhood settings. Leaders give members a description of a hypothetical social situation, act the part of the other child who is present in the situation, and ask them to act out what they think they would say or do. One situation is as follows: "Let's pretend you made plans to meet your friend Chris after school. When you go outside a classmate tells you that Chris left with someone else. The next day in school you see your friend Chris." Leaders assess and use group work to enhance members' problem-solving abilities. Underlying group work is the assumption that members with low levels of social competence have cognitive deficits in their ability to solve interpersonal problems. Some interpersonal-cognitive problem-solving (ICPS) skills are directly related to members' social adjustment (Spivack et al., 1976).

The cognitive elements of social competence relate to six ICPS skills, namely members' ways of thinking about and resolving their social difficulties, which should be assessed and developed through group work. Members' sensitivity to, awareness of, and responsiveness to their own and others' feelings underlie all ICPS skills and are required for reciprocal and supportive social relationships to develop. The first ICPS skill is members' sensitivity to the existence of interpersonal problems. Members who are aware of interpersonal difficulties are in a good position to think of how to resolve such difficulties. Through group discussion it became apparent to the leaders and some of the members that Kate often was unaware of her friends' ideas and moods. One of the leaders suggested that Kate ask her friends about their thoughts and feelings more frequently. Although Kate initially resisted the idea, in a later session she reported that she had tried to do so more often with her friends.

A second skill is members' consideration of alternatives. Subsequent to formulating the interpersonal problem, the members think of different ways of solving it. Adolescent members often are better able to think of alternatives or choices and may require less skill development than younger members. In an adolescent group held at a community center, Rob mentioned that Alex, a boy in his class, had kicked in his briefcase at school. The members came up with many alternatives, including talking to his parents, telling his teacher, talking to Alex, trying to make friends with Alex, and talking to friends in the class.

A third skill is adolescent members' thinking of potential consequences to potential solutions, which is useful in sorting out the value of each alternative prior to implementing one. Rob pondered his alternatives and considered that if he brought the subject up with his father he might listen. He knew that his mother would be concerned about his safety. If Rob talked to his teacher she might talk to Alex or Alex's parents. In thinking about whether to talk to Alex, Rob realized he didn't understand what made Alex smash in his briefcase. Also, Rob was angry with Alex and didn't want to or know how to be friends with him. Rob couldn't readily talk to the kids in the class because they would think he wasn't standing up to Alex.

A fourth ICPS skill is decision making, which includes members' ability to select the alternative with the best chance of being effective. Potentially, all members are able to make sound decisions. Although Rob wanted the members to decide which alternative to choose, with the leaders' guidance they insisted that he decide. Although Rob talked in the group about approaching the boy directly, he first talked things over with his father.

A fifth skill involves members' considering how to attain a social or interpersonal objective. The ability to plan steps, or means-ends problem-solving thinking, although often present to some degree among members, can be exercised in the group. Marcia was a very lonely girl. With the help of the group, Marcia decided on several strategies to make friends with two girls in her class. Marcia decided to play together more closely during recess with Tina and tried approaching Tina more often at school. Marcia thought that it would be good to call up Nikki and invite her to come over to her house to play.

Social competence varies developmentally, such that what is skillful for younger members is likely to be considered unskillful for older ones. Indeed, the social and emotional developmental level of children and adolescents serve as an upper boundary for their skill acquisition. Older members tend to be more socially responsive and skillful and have more advanced peer interactions than younger members (Vandell & Mueller, 1980). Many adolescent members are able to think abstractly about social interaction. Due to their greater maturity, adolescents have the potential to encompass more factors and be more complex in regard to their problem-solving thinking skills than children. A sixth skill is adolescent members' ability to realize the reciprocal nature of their social interactions. Furthermore, the complexities related to biological development change the nature, quality, and type of adolescents' social relationships. In an adolescent group, Ann mentioned that every time she began to talk to her friend Rowena about her problems with boys, Rowena had a tendency to talk to her about having the same problems. Ann found that when she listened to Rowena then Rowena would listen to her.

The group is used to develop members' abilities to effectively conceptualize solutions to commonly experienced difficulties. The leaders conduct discussions and role plays of hypothetical situations and stories involving youngsters with whom the members can readily identify. For instance, the leaders present a story in which a child is on his way to school and a youngster threatens him. The leaders and members develop an array of alternatives to creatively solve the problems that are discussed.

Through playing games, which represent practice applications, members develop their problem-solving skills (Elardo & Cooper, 1977). For instance, in one board game the members take turns landing on spaces each of which is labeled with an emotion. The member then describes a social situation that he or she recently has experienced that evoked the emotion. Marguerite landed on "mad." She said, "I told a friend of mine a secret that I asked her not to tell anybody else. Yesterday another girl told me that Donna told her what I said." Marguerite and the members then discussed how to resolve the problem.

Leaders may conduct social skills training by identifying and ameliorating members' problems in social performance. By elementary school, children develop a skill repertory that if unsatisfactory requires group work to change it (Barclay, 1966).

Role plays help members increase their repertoire of social skills. They rehearse their performance in difficult social situations. Leaders conduct problem-focused discussions at several points during role plays, namely during the analysis of the problem situation brought in by a member, during the consideration of alternative ways to act in the problem situation, and again following the reflection on the role playing performed by the member. To develop social skills, leaders introduce games that involve observation, dramatics, and discussion. In one game, a member is chosen and a card is temporarily attached to the member's back. The card identifies the member as either a bully, best friend, new child in class, shy child, happy child, or sad child. The members act toward the member who is "it" as if the latter were the character on the card. The member who is "it" then guesses which role she or he is playing.

PLANNING AND COMPOSITION

Most social competence groups are highly structured and require a considerable amount of planning. Often, an equivalent amount of time and effort goes into planning as into implementation.

Before actual selection of members begins, leaders develop criteria for the selection of appropriate members to provide commonality and unity to the group. Although social competence groups are often homogeneous in gender and age (Huey, 1983), some leaders have had success with mixed-gender groups (McCullagh, 1981).

Leaders often plan to construct groups of members who can mutually benefit from their varying levels of social competence. Such groups have some members with high levels of social competence, some who have some difficulties, and some who have many difficulties.

At times leaders form competence groups whose main purpose is primary prevention. Such groups are composed to be similar to or part of school and community system groups in which youngsters regularly participate. For social competence groups whose main purpose is either secondary or tertiary prevention, leaders include members who clearly have peer relationship difficulties.

After the leaders have developed their criteria they seek referrals. On the basis of referrals that they have received, the leaders develop a list of potential members. Through interviewing potential members, leaders assess their level of social competence and suitability for membership. Then, the leaders select the actual group members.

Prior to the first group, session leaders determine the length of the group in regard to time and number of sessions. They prepare an outline for each session that includes skill objectives, such activities as role plays and games, and materials required for conducting the group, such as pencils and cards. For instance, the objectives of an adolescent group session may be as follows: Develop alternative and consequential problem-solving thinking in regard to situations arising with peers.

LEADERSHIP AND ACTIVITIES

Leaders demonstrate and apply human relations skills that serve as exemplars for the members who observe them. They promote social interaction among the members in a friendly manner. To promote social skills development among members the leaders may transfer some of their functions to them.

Many social competence groups are co-led and involve the careful delineation of respective roles. Collaboration and communication prior to, during, and between sessions ensure smooth process. To guide their own professional development, junior or relatively inexperienced leaders tend to rely on supervision and feedback from senior leaders and supervisors.

To promote solidarity, most social competence groups focus on the achievement of group-level objectives that are shared by the members, such as the acquisition of knowledge about problem solving in interpersonal situations. In addition, many social competence groups allow for the specification of and progress toward attaining individual-level objectives, which are specific to particular members.

Leaders use activities that are natural components of the social lives of children and adolescents to promote the peer relationships and social competence of members. Leaders employ role playing to promote members' social development. Through role playing, members increase their perspective-taking ability, empathy, and understanding of the viewpoints of other persons. Many members readily participate in and benefit from role playing. Role-play activities have been shown to be effective in helping depressed members become more socially involved (Stark et al., 1991) and in assisting anxious members in acquiring coping skills (Kendall et al., 1992; Ollendick & Francis, 1988). Role playing varies in regard to degree of structure, centrality in programming, and linkage to practice components. In group work that emphasizes social skills development, role playing is a requisite and major component. It tends to be a highly structured multistep procedure involving situations that stem from members' actual life experiences. In contrast, in group work that emphasizes interpersonal-cognitive problem solving, role playing is often an optional and minor component. It tends to be moderately structured, involving hypothetical situations that are discussed in the group.

Leaders use discussion, which broadens the limited experience of each member, to promote an understanding of problem-solving ideas. Discussions tend to be moderately ordered in regard to the norms governing participation and the sequence and timing of topics. In ongoing discussions the group considers topics over multiple sessions. In the middle and ending phases, discussions promote the application of knowledge and skills to situations that demand social competence.

In social competence groups for adolescents, leaders conduct abstract discussions of problem-solving principles and present general concepts that transcend the situations and details discussed in earlier phases. In contrast to discussions with adolescents, most discussions with young children tend to be concrete.

Some discussions are related to crises in the group as a whole or to personal crises experienced by individual members, with the likelihood of the occurrence of the discussions being in direct relation to the degree of difficulties experienced by the group and the individual members. For instance, in a tertiary prevention group held at a community center, several developmentally disabled members were upset about changes in the meal plan. The group discussions led to a session with the program director, who attempted to explain the changes to the members.

As an element of play, games contribute to the social development of members. Members of social competence groups tend to use their knowledge of and skill in game playing to develop their peer relationships (LeCroy, 1987). Games promote an atmosphere of enjoyment, spontaneity, and creativity. Whereas some games may be brief, elaborate problem-solving games, such as AWARE-O (Elardo & Cooper, 1977, pp. 180-182), may consume an entire session.

Sessions are structured in regard to purpose, activity, and intended outcome. In the beginning phase, the leaders provide an orientation, cooperatively establish the rules, and discuss the purposes as related to friendships. Members who are or become acquainted usually develop a name for the group. In the middle phase the sessions are devoted to the development of cognitive skills, with each session emphasizing a limited number of skills.

The leaders promote an overall understanding of the problem-solving approach and its application to the development of social competence. In the ending phase, the final sessions are devoted to bringing in friends, holding sessions elsewhere, fading out the group, and simultaneously strengthening the connection of members to school and community systems.

AN EXAMPLE: AUTUMN,
WINTER, SPRING, AND SUMMER

A consortium of professionals organized a social competence development program that linked higher education institutions with elementary schools. The program staff consisted of faculty and graduate students in educational psychology, counseling, and social work who were interested in promoting the social competence of young children. After a year of development work, consisting of reviewing professional literature, designing an intervention, and considering possible intervention sites, the program staff approached a medium-sized local parochial elementary school with an offer to provide social competence group work. The program staff presented a workshop at which they described typical social competence difficulties of school-age children, the importance and consequence of such difficulties, and means for remediation. The school staff readily could relate to descriptions of children who were shy and those who knew no other means of dealing with conflict other than fighting. Nonetheless, they lacked familiarity with terms, such as social competence. "What's that?" asked one of the participants. "So what if a kid has no friends?" asked another and then, referring to herself, added, "I got over it." The school administrators, who found good interpersonal relationships consistent with their religious perspective, were receptive to the presentation. It became clear to the program staff that the school administrators were more interested in a preventive program than an intervention program. The administrators mentioned the case of Lawrence, a former student at their school, who had not shown any signs of difficulty they could discern yet became a heroin addict. The administrators understood that providing preventive services to younger children was potentially most beneficial.

After a series of discussions about children, classes, and teachers, the program staff and the school administrators agreed to implement a preventive social competence group work program in the third grade. The administrators indicated that several potential social competence difficulties seemed to be appearing among the third-grade children. They described incidents of quarreling in the cafeteria that were worrisome to them. The program staff and the school administrators were convinced that third-grade children were mature enough to grasp cognitive material presented in a preventive group. The principal discussed the ideas for a social competence development program with the three third-grade teachers who appeared to be amenable to a classroom approach. Nonetheless, one of the teachers delayed implementing any planning activities for such an approach, always coming up with another reason why he could not do it. The program staff then considered the other classroom teachers. The teacher who most enthusiastically supported such a program left before it could be implemented. The preventive program was delivered in Marta's classroom.

Using a preventive approach in the classroom had several advantages in the school. Although the school staff were aware of the social competence difficulties of several third-grade children, the latter were not singled out for treatment and therefore were not stigmatized. Staff members were able to reach children who appeared to require intervention, as well as others, in a genteel fashion.

The teacher's role included the coordination of program content with the rest of the curriculum, such as social studies and health education. The program content focused on increasing empathy, promoting a positive self-concept, and learning to analyze and apply problem-solving thinking skills in social situations involving peers. Prior to delivering the program, the leaders discussed the content and approach with the school staff who, after a brief delay, indicated their approval.

The teacher provided the leaders with a class list that was complete except for the inclusion of Julio, a newly arrived Spanish-speaking boy. All parents were informed about the program through a letter the teacher sent home. Virtually all parents agreed to the program. One mother spoke to the principal, who reassured her. The children were also willing participants. The leaders came one day to observe the class and to their surprise they saw several children acting aggressively toward their peers. During recess, one boy pushed Julio down onto the concrete of the school playground. Julio's knee required attention from the school nurse. His new green pants were ruined. The following day Julio appeared with the same pants, which had a patch on them.

The class was divided into four smaller groups, each of which met in a corner of the classroom. Each group selected a member who chose a name of a season out of a hat. Two of the groups exchanged names with one another. The children were comfortable with the room and were accustomed to working in groups. The groups met once a week for 12 weeks.

Most of the pupils had been in the same school since they began their studies. They already knew one another from the classroom, and cohesiveness was present. In the beginning phase, the leaders provided the members with an orientation to the program and set expectations and group goals. One leader described the program to the children as learning about friendship. The children were asked their goals for the group. Most repeated what the leader had already said; however, some members voiced their concerns about fighting. One girl described a shocking incident in which two kids had a fight in the hallway and pulled each other's hair, scattered each other's books and papers, and scratched and bit each other.

The members learned to identify, describe, and express their feelings to each other and be more empathic to others. They played a board game the leaders had developed in which they each had to say what they felt in common school situations, including the weekly all-school assembly. To the surprise of one of the leaders, one of the members described her discomfort at being in the assembly and other large groups. Indeed, the member was ultimately referred for a mental health assessment. The members role played social situations and practiced responding in kindness to one another. One of the situations that was role played was one in which a boy was always the last one chosen to be on a team. Ultimately, he decided to practice extensively and became a very good athlete.

Educational and social-recreational activities were combined and accepted by the members. The children were aware that the group was classlike. Nonetheless, they also realized and later commented that they played more games and had more opportunities to discuss personal topics in the group than they did in their regular class.

In the middle phase, the members developed their assertiveness skills by practicing making appropriate requests of peers. As each class group was composed of children with a range of social abilities (from unassertive to assertive to aggressive) there were many opportunities for role playing and modeling. The leaders helped members learn to relate feelings to actions by describing events and how they felt about them. Such events were used to develop role-playing scenarios. A member described a situation in which he had arranged to go bike riding with a friend, but when he showed up at the appointed place in the nearby park his friend was not there.

In one activity the members verbalized positive characteristics about themselves. Some children enjoyed bragging to each other about their accomplishments, although the shy children had a difficult time with the activity. When children had difficulty thinking of or saying positive things about themselves the leaders and other members gave them some ideas. Jack blushed profusely when others complimented him about his consideration of others. Apparently, he was not used to receiving compliments at home, at school, or in the neighborhood.

The members focused on social skills involved in making and keeping friends. They practiced initiating and maintaining conversations.

The quiet members appeared to learn from the louder ones, yet despite much practice they continued to say little in the group. It seemed to the leaders that the quiet members might always have difficulty making friends.

Members learned conflict identification and resolution skills and practiced using problem-solving thinking in stressful situations involving the aggressive actions of peers. The members described a situation in which high school boys had come to their school and had attempted to enter the locked gates. Many children were frightened and those who received advance word of the event had managed to leave school early.

The final phase emphasized consolidating gains, evaluating the group, and ending. The members reviewed how to apply problem-solving thinking to conflict situations involving peers. For instance, some members discussed how to handle a situation in which another child who was a stranger attempted to obtain money from them. Members discussed their abilities to understand problematic situations and several reported improved peer relationships. Afterward, the teacher related the lessons learned to the overall social studies curriculum, which was focused on the theme of people in the natural world. The following year another third-grade classroom benefited by the experience. The teacher consulted with Marta, the teacher in whose classroom the program had been implemented, in order to use the preventive group work approach to promoting social competence.

CONCLUSION

Group work can be used to develop the social competence and peer relationships of members. Social competence groups have the potential to improve members' skills at making and keeping friends, getting along with others, and increasing acceptance by peers. They are also a means of reducing members' shyness, isolation, neglect, and rejection.

Sufficient time must be devoted to reach such objectives. Structured time-limited social competence groups are likely to produce modest yet rapid improvements in a few areas. To improve their chances of success, leaders clearly tailor composition to the purpose and type of social competence group.

Leaders attempt to develop members' cognitive skills, which have the potential for applicability in diverse social situations. They promote social competence that is valued within group, school, and community systems and that will be useful for the youngsters.

Whereas some gains may persist over a longer period of time, considerably more programmatic development will ensure that consolidation and application of gains takes place. Schoolwide and communitywide competence-building programs are likely to enhance the effectiveness of the group work program in improving the social competence of children and adolescents.

This chapter has focused on group work for social competence and peer relationship difficulties. In the next chapter we will explicate the use of group work for promoting the mental health of children and adolescents.

Chapter 8

MENTAL HEALTH
AND SUBSTANCE ABUSE

MENTAL HEALTH AND SUBSTANCE
ABUSE AS A SOCIAL PROBLEM

The purpose of this chapter is to consider how leaders can use group work to ameliorate the mental health and substance abuse problems of children and adolescents. The impact of mental health and substance abuse difficulties on children and adolescents is evident in the suffering experienced by youngsters and their families, the burden and cost of care, and the social disruption experienced in communities (Christian, Henderson, Morse, & Wilson, 1983).

Given that youngsters who are busy coping with mental disorders and substance abuse difficulties have less resources of time and energy to spend on school activities, it is apparent that such problems tend to interfere with learning and school performance (Beaudoin, 1991; Newton-Logsdon & Armstrong, 1993; see Chapter 9). Mental health and substance abuse problems have the potential to change the self-concept of children and adolescents, the course of their studies, their career objectives, and their interpersonal relationships and may result in placement in special schools and special education programs (Harper & Shillito, 1991).

Mental disorders that are usually first diagnosed in infancy, childhood, or adolescence include learning disorders as well as more commonly recognized or traditional mental disorders (American Psychiatric Association, 1994). In special education, group work is used to help children with learning disorders, such as those pertaining to reading, mathematics, and written expression. Youngsters with mild and moderate levels of mental retardation are more likely to attend school and participate in group work programs in community systems. Youngsters with attention-deficit and disruptive behavior disorders, including attention-deficit hyperactivity disorder (ADHD), conduct disorder, and oppositional defiant disorder, also can be helped in group work programs (Daratha, 1992; Rauch et al., 1987; Richert, 1986; Timmer, 1995). Members with ADHD may benefit from highly structured groups with clear and consistent rules and expectations (Mueller, 1993). Leaders use cognitive therapy, including self-talk, to reduce impulsiveness and behavioral therapy, including positive reinforcement for appropriate responses.

Substance abuse is a major problem for many adolescents. Adolescent substance abuse can adversely influence identity, self-concept, peer affiliations, and physical development (Wodarski, 1988). Dual mental health and substance abuse disorders commonly covary among adolescents, who are usually treated for such problems in community mental health and substance abuse treatment centers.

PURPOSE OF GROUP WORK

Group work aims at reducing risk factors that contribute to the development and exacerbation of mental health and substance abuse disorders. Emotional and mental well-being are important objectives of group work programs, which are useful in teaching children and adolescents how to cope with stress and anxiety (Shields, 1985).

Crisis intervention, including reducing cognitive dissonance and conducting problem-solving discussions, is useful in helping members cope with highly stressful situations that can result in mental health emergencies and posttraumatic stress disorder (PTSD; Pope, Campbell, & Kurtz, 1992). In a middle school support group for victims of PTSD, the leaders emphasized providing a rationale for the group, setting rules, and establishing rapport among the members, in the beginning phase. The leaders used active listening skills focusing on warmth, empathy, and genuineness, and encouraged bonding and trust. In the middle phase, the leaders supported, in concept and application, the members' willingness to take risks and express their feelings.

The leaders used ventilation and recapitulation of the crisis, role modeling, relaxation training, guided imagery, and cognitive restructuring. In the end phase, the leaders enabled the members to apply the skills they had learned to their daily lives and encouraged them to provide one another with constructive feedback and to express their feelings about termination.

By providing a setting in which members discuss concerns, issues, and experiences, mental health group work provides support and understanding to members. The sense of belonging and acceptance that is part of the supportive group is crucial to promoting youngsters' sense of well-being (Golner, 1983). Adolescent support groups provide members with opportunities to improve their abilities to think clearly and objectively, test their assumptions, and receive corrective feedback about consuming alcohol and using other drugs (Schwebel, 1992).

Group work can help reduce the stigma associated with mental disorder and substance abuse (Berkovitz, 1989). Concomitantly, children or adolescents with substance abuse disorders are helped to admit that they have a problem, which is often a preliminary step in dealing with such problems.

Primary prevention group work is intended to obviate the development of mental health and substance disorders among children and adolescents and consequently reduce the demand for later intervention. Primary prevention is particularly valuable when it is offered to many youngsters. Leaders are likely to find many young children in school and community systems who are free of disorders. Primary prevention involves reaching adolescents at a time when they are likely to become exposed to situations that could endanger their mental well-being and that could cause them to develop mental health disorders. Primary prevention actions in group work include teaching members alternatives and refusals to taking drugs offered by peers. Leaders use modeling processes to provide adolescent members with exemplars of how to resist pressures to engage in substance abuse.

Secondary prevention group work with children and adolescents who have recently recognized mild or moderate mental disorders is prevalent (Carroll, 1980). Its aims include forestalling future deterioration of the mental health of members, lessening the impact of or eliminating the disorder, teaching members to cope with the disorder, and promoting understanding of and reducing stigma associated with the disorder. Secondary prevention activities include the provision of group psychotherapy.

The purpose of tertiary prevention group work is the rehabilitation of children and adolescents who are severely or persistently influenced by a mental disorder or substance abuse. Whereas the aims of tertiary prevention are often limited to maintaining members at their current, minimal level of functioning, the purposes also can include the rehabilitation of mentally disabled and handicapped youngsters to provide them with a better level of functioning, as in special education classrooms. Tertiary prevention activities in groups include teaching youngsters with severe mental illness to recognize when they are decompensating or are actively hallucinating or delusional.

PROBLEM RECOGNITION AND SOLUTION

Mental health and substance abuse disorders vary in terms of the degree to which they are publicly perceived and privately experienced, their levels of acceptability and stigmatization, and the degree to which they evoke sympathy. Whereas some disorders are readily recognized, others are known only to the youngster. Youngsters who feel shame about a problem may be unwilling to reveal it and indeed may conceal their difficulty. Older children and adolescents tend to be more likely to detect and comprehend their own mental health problems than young children.

The detection of and communication about mental health problems is influenced by youngsters' family structures, peer group networks, and the extent to which they have access to health care providers. Whereas young children are likely to communicate such concerns within their immediate family, many adolescents are as likely to discuss such concerns with close friends as they are with family members (Windle, Miller-Tutzauer, Barnes, & Welte, 1991). Although most adolescent peer groups promote mental health, one type tends to put the adolescent at greater risk for developing mental health problems (Downs & Rose,

1991; Rose & Downs, 1989). Members of the high-risk peer group tend to underestimate the hazards of substance abuse. Recognition of individual adolescents with mental health problems is associated with their participation in a peer group consisting of many individuals with such problems.

Whereas many school and community officials are aware of the occurrence of mental disorders and substance abuse in populations of children and adolescents, their recognition of mental health problems among particular youngsters with whom they interact varies according to their professional education and experience. Many educators recognize and are alert to the problems of learning disabilities. Pupil-personnel-services practitioners in schools are often likely to detect mental disorders and substance abuse difficulties.

The understanding of individuals in community systems contributes to the successful establishment and implementation of group work. In some communities backing is available for preventive and educational group work, whereas in others interventive and remediational group work is more acceptable (Carroll, 1980; Golner, 1983). Support groups, including 12-step programs, are useful in helping children of alcoholic and substance-abusing parents and serving adolescent alcohol or substance abusers (Sprang, 1989). Adolescent members of groups for children of alcoholics often report difficulty in problem solving (Bogdaniak & Piercy, 1987). Many are confused, scared, and upset about the unpredictable, inconsistent, and inappropriate behavior of their alcoholic parents, which can include violence, crimes, and inappropriate sexual conduct. Group work with adolescent children of alcoholics often begins with a consideration of the recognition, differentiation, and acceptance of problems (Hanson & Liber, 1989). Leaders proceed to develop members' communication skills through distinguishing between passive and active listening skills and between passive, assertive, and aggressive behaviors.

Community systems influence the availability and type of mental health group work provided in school systems. In school systems, parents or legal guardians give their permission for participation of children in group work programs that are offered beyond the regular school curriculum of subjects, such as physical and health education.

School-based clinics provide group work for mental health care. Treatment and psychotherapy groups for emotionally disturbed children and for drug-addicted adolescents are offered in regular and special schools (Berkovitz, 1989). Leaders use screening tests to detect mental disorders and substance abuse and obtain information pertaining to mental health group work. Useful instruments include the Behavior Rating Index for Children, Depression Self-Rating Scale, Eyberg Child Behavior Inventory, Hopelessness Scale for Children, Hospital Fears Rating Scale, Multi-Attitude Suicide Tendency Scale, and the Revised Behavior Problem Checklist (Fischer & Corcoran, 1994; Quay & Peterson, 1983). Some practical instruments for assessing variables related to alcoholism include the Adolescent Alcohol Questionnaire (Gliksman, Smythe, Gorman, & Rush, 1980) and the Behavioral Analysis Questionnaire for Adolescent Drinkers (Stumphauzer, 1980).

The problem-solving process continues following problem recognition and assessment. Group work with children and adolescents involves identifying and ameliorating problems. Usually, leaders perceive more of the multiple problems that are associated with having a mental or substance abuse disorder than do the members with the disorder. In short-term groups, leaders directly identify problems that can be focused on for contracted activity designed to reach a solution (Shields, 1985). Subsequent to identifying the disorders, the leaders use the problem-solving process in specifying and working toward helping the group attain prevention and intervention goals (Breidenbach, 1984).

The type of mental health or substance abuse disorder influences the purpose and mode of group work. Group work with members with learning disabilities consists of a combination of support and academic skill interventions that are aimed at increasing their emotional and instrumental functional capacities. Group work with adolescents who grew up with parental alcoholism begins with a getting acquainted exercise and proceeds to members drawing a genogram and discussing their families (Rohde & Stockton, 1993).

Then, leaders use a cognitive approach by providing members with information about alcoholism. In a later session, members arrive at a more rational and accurate view of their thoughts, feelings, and experiences. Subsequently, they learn assertive communication skills, role play family situations, and practice decision-making skills. Finally, they share what they liked most about the group and what they gained.

PLANNING AND COMPOSITION

Ideally, planning encompasses fact-finding activities to determine the incidence and prevalence of mental health problems that are manifest in populations of children and adolescents within particular school and community systems. Usually such knowledge is more readily available when it is regularly collected, for instance, as a component of a larger project. Leaders who are able to acquire such knowledge either on a formal or informal basis are then better able to consider what types of groups may be formed.

Time is an important planning consideration. Leaders of time-limited groups decide in advance how many sessions will be held and the length of each session. Given the attention, concentration, and memory patterns of young children, they are best served by frequent, brief sessions that are held at least, ideally, more than once a week.

In planning mental health promoting activities for young members, leaders determine which, how, and when play materials are to be used. Members increase their awareness of hazards to their mental health through engaging in play scenarios. Activities with adolescents include more sophisticated role-playing strategies than tend to be used with young children and more elaborate and in-depth discussions about concerns particular to their age group, such as substance abuse and suicide (Stillion, McDowell, & May, 1989; Trautman & Shaffer, 1984).

Planning for work with members who have mental disorders consists of preparation for interaction with them as individuals and as a group. Leaders prepare by examining their own reactions as well as by being prepared to deal with the reactions of members (Schwartz, 1961, 1971). Many mental disorders induce a mixture of emotional reactions in members and leaders ranging from fear and anxiety to sympathy and understanding. Members vary in the extent to which they are aware of, label, and identify their emotional reactions. Leaders plan group work to enhance members' knowledge of their own reactions.

Composition is a key factor in the ultimate effectiveness of the group. Primary prevention groups are composed so that few if any members have identified mental health or substance abuse difficulties, and secondary and tertiary prevention groups are composed such that all members have identified difficulties.

In community systems with large numbers of children or adolescents with a particular disorder, it is feasible for leaders to construct one or more groups with members who have such a disorder in common. In such groups a trend toward unity, cohesion, and support exists. Open, in-depth sharing and discussion of feelings and problems among older children and adolescents also is viable (Stevenson, 1986). Leaders also may compose supportive groups of members who have a range of disorders. It is also feasible to compose groups of members who have mental and physical disorders (Kennedy, 1989).

Care is to be taken in composing groups that consist primarily of adolescents with mental disorders or who are engaging in substance abuse. To achieve an optimum group climate, leaders balance membership in regard to age, gender, level of sophistication, intelligence, and personality style (Scheidlinger, 1985).

When significant mental health problems are present among the members, sufficient instrumental and emotional support must be made available to them (Curran, 1987). Furthermore, the leaders should carefully monitor the mental status and well-being of the youngsters. For example, in a secondary prevention group of adolescents two members had made suicide attempts. The leaders were particularly concerned that one young adolescent might again make an attempt, particularly as a girl in her class recently had made such an attempt. They inaugurated an intensive series of individual and family sessions that complemented the group work activities.

Many groups focus on one rather than on both sets of problems of dually diagnosed adolescents. In such instances the leaders must be aware of potential difficulties that may arise in regard to the difficulty that is receiving less attention. For instance, in a secondary prevention group that focused on substance abuse disorders, one adolescent, Nikki, also had an eating disorder.

Nikki was referred to a bulimia treatment group that provided her with psychoeducation, movement therapy, and self-help and examined eating, nutrition, and postmeal activities (Eliot, 1990; Harper & Shillito, 1991; Johnson & Connors, 1987).

In many instances, groups for adolescents that focus on identified problems other than mental health have some members who either have diagnosable mental disorders or are involved in substance abuse. Such members may be receiving care for such difficulties outside the context of the group.

Youngsters who receive group work for mental health or substance abuse difficulties often receive additional services outside of the group. It behooves the leaders to be aware of all services received by members to coordinate and understand their impact on the members. Leaders also will consider the possibility of using group work in conjunction and coordination with individual, parent, and family counseling, socialization and recreational activities, and crisis intervention (Birmingham, 1986; Christian et al., 1983). Indeed, group work with adolescents in school and community systems is often preceded by individual counseling (Scheidlinger, 1985).

LEADERSHIP AND ACTIVITIES

Through the use of their own professional knowledge, as well as that of guest speakers, and the knowledge of experts as represented in written and audiovisual materials, the leaders provide information to the members about mental health and substance abuse topics (LeCoq & Capuzzi, 1984). Leaders must be careful to balance perspectives and discussions of mental illness and disability with those of mental health and strength. The purpose and approach of the presentation of material varies in accordance with the preventive level. In primary prevention groups, information is presented with the purpose of preventing mental health and substance abuse problems. A public health approach allows the leaders to provide the members with factual information that shows the dangers that mental health and substance abuse problems may pose for them in the future. In secondary prevention groups, information is presented to overcome actual difficulties and restore prior functioning. The leaders reassure the members that it is within their reach to improve their mental health and reduce their substance abuse. In tertiary prevention groups, information is presented to help members maintain their level of functioning and prevent deterioration. The leaders encourage the members to participate in their own mental health self-care. The provision of mental health and substance abuse information is usually in conformity to the norms of school and community systems. For instance, in one group of adolescent girls held at a parochial school, the members discussed dating relationships. Nonetheless, limits were placed on the degree of detailed information that was provided about certain birth control measures.

In secondary and tertiary prevention groups, leaders focus on limitations due to the disorder, self-concept related to the disorder, and labeling by and reactions of other persons to the disorder (Wodarski, 1988). Leaders attempt to improve members' confidence, self-esteem, good feelings about themselves, and motivation (Beare, 1991; Brown & Kingsley, 1975). They emphasize issues, such as winning and losing, which are closely tied to the members' self-esteem, through competitive physical games, including races, tugs of war, and volleyball, followed by structured cooperative games, including a balloon-toss game (Richert, 1986).

Collaboration between coleaders involves consultations and discussions prior to and following the sessions. The leaders maintain a harmonious working relationship, secure agreement about how to proceed with leading the group, and exchange information. Whereas coleadership in group work generally involves two professionals, innovations include a partnership between a professional leader and a parent (Eliot, 1990) and the use of as many as four leaders to provide maximum emotional support and informational feedback (Stengel, 1987).

Leadership varies according to the development of the group. In the beginning phase, the leaders establish norms of acceptance to counter the stigma that some members may experience owing to societal reactions to their disorder (Shields, 1985). The leaders permit members to vent their anger. By the middle phase and continuing into the ending phase, members are encouraged to take a more active role in contributing to the group and helping each other solve problems (Birmingham, 1986).

As cohesion increases in the group, trust and disclosure also tend to increase. In most groups a moderate amount of disclosure is desirable.

Nonetheless, if a great deal of disclosure occurs, the nature of the process and indeed the type of group may change. At times, group work with members who are dealing with mental disorders that are distressing to them has a tendency to become psychotherapeutic. The qualities and style of the interactions between and among the members and the leaders varies according to the characteristics of the disorder that are addressed. Depression and grief groups are usually cathartic and comforting. They can help members with depressive disorders receive support and engage in activities that can help them improve their moods (Fine et al., 1991). For older adolescents more attention is likely to be paid to the concept of depression itself and explicit means of alleviating it. Leaders who use the positive group technique request depressed adolescents to make only positive statements about themselves and other group members, to acknowledge received compliments, and to refrain from making negative comments (Holmes & Wagner, 1992). The Adolescent Coping With Depression Course is a skills workshop for teaching members to relax, increase pleasant events and social competence, communicate, negotiate, resolve conflict, and control negative thoughts (Clarke & Lewinsohn, 1989).

Frequently, groups composed of adolescents with substance abuse disorders have a ceremony or ritual for acknowledging the disorder. Leaders may use incident drawings to overcome members' denial of difficulties (Cox & Price, 1990). At times, when adolescents are unwilling to acknowledge their substance abuse difficulty the process can become confrontative. For other disorders, it is also often helpful for the members to admit having a certain difficulty. Such disclosure and acknowledgment practices are common in both short-term and long-term groups.

Several activities enhance adolescents' involvement in the group and alleviate anxiety. Adolescent members may prepare, serve, and enjoy a snack, which allows them to feel welcome and to satisfy their appetite (Stengel, 1987). Physical activities and games include exercising with music, playing monkey in the middle, playing basketball, jogging, and bowling.

Usually, leaders adopt an informal tone, use language that is suitable for communicating with members, and avoid professional jargon. Leaders often use simpler words with children than with adolescents. With adolescents, leaders' choice of language is often fairly close to that of adult speech. Some leaders choose to include occasional adolescent language phrases. Nonetheless, adult leaders are wise to avoid trying to speak entirely in the style of the members.

The leaders directly define the purpose of the group and set the expectations for the members in the initial sessions of the early phase. They use an inductive approach to introduce the members to problem solving. For children, problem solving may be presented in a gamelike format along with discussion. For adolescents the approach is more likely to be tied to a presentation and discussion of examples and applications involving their peers.

The group proceeds rapidly to the more extensive middle phase. Members develop alternative means to solve their problems and may role play each alternative (Rauch et al., 1987). Members decide on a particular solution, set it in motion, and then report back on its consequences in a subsequent session. Leaders may have to help members who have considerable difficulties in comprehending or implementing some aspects of the sequence.

As the early phase, the ending phase tends to be briefer than the middle phase. The later sessions are devoted to trying out innovative problem-solving strategies and applying them to members' school and community systems, elaborately reviewing and summarizing problem solving, and evaluating the success of the group. The group completes all of its tasks and provides members with a sense of closure (LeCoq & Capuzzi, 1984). Adolescent members may discuss how substance use may keep them from achieving their life goals. Members express their appreciation and give and receive positive feedback. Feedback should be descriptive, specific, solicited, well timed, accurate, and clearly communicated. Feedback should take into account both the receiver and giver of feedback and should be directed toward actions within the control of the receiver.

Leaders can consult with school staff to identify members who are vulnerable to termination due to past losses and conduct workshops for parents, teachers, administrators, and pupil-personnel-service staff to permit exploration of termination issues (Morse, Bartolotta, Cushman, & Rubin, 1982). Vulnerable members can benefit from individual or additional group work, classroom meetings, and written assignments that focus on termination issues (Webb, 1993). Group work for children who have lost a peer due to suicide include leader actions for intervening early, identifying the immediate survivor group, reviewing the life and death of the deceased, shaping expectations of funeral ceremonies and shaping group ritual response, supporting survivorship status of the larger organization (i.e., the school and community system), and providing a complete academic autopsy (Zinner, 1987).

AN EXAMPLE: kNOw DOPES

In a rural midwestern community, four boys ages 14 to 17 stole a Ford van belonging to the county senior citizens' center, speedily drove into a neighboring town, and proceeded to drink late into the night. The three older boys coerced Joel, the youngest one, to drink so heavily that he died. The bar where this illicit activity occurred was closed and its owners were fined. A month-long police investigation ensued as well as a major state inquiry into adolescent substance abuse.

As a consequence of the tragedy of Joel's highly publicized death, public health officials, nurses, and physicians became more aware of adolescent substance abuse in the schools and in the county. A meeting was held at which community and civic officials discussed what could be done to prevent adolescent substance abuse. Community leaders made inquiries at state headquarters of their civic organizations and ultimately decided on using a program development consultant.

After gathering information about the demographic characteristics and social service requirements of the county, the consultant drafted a plan that had several recommendations, including the proposed formation of a primary prevention group on substance abuse issues for young adolescents. The consultant presented the plan at a meeting of regional middle schools and high schools. It was ratified at a subsequent meeting of the civic steering committee. Subsequently, committee members obtained the cooperation of the principal, the teachers, and the parents' organizations at both schools.

A local practitioner, who served as a group leader, developed the consultant's plan. To secure broader support for the proposal, the leader made introductory phone calls to community leaders. Most of the parents who attended a meeting held by the leader to discuss the proposed group thought it was a good idea. The group was scheduled to meet Tuesdays after school for one semester. The leader secured a community room at the easily accessible local shopping mall as a meeting place for the group. The group was widely advertised and many health, civic, and school officials actively promoted it. To make attendance feasible, registration, which was offered on a first come, first serve basis, was scheduled one month in advance of the actual group sessions.

The beginning sessions were devoted to getting acquainted and becoming oriented to the purpose of the group. Of the dozen adolescents who registered, 10 came to the first session. At the first session, Patrick, who was unwilling to discuss substance abuse concerns with peers in a group, was offered an individual appointment, which he refused. Apparently, he continued to attend school with no indications of substance abuse activity, which surprised the leader.

Of the nine members who remained, five, who attended the same regional high school, were well acquainted. The other members included Andres, who had newly arrived in the community from Mexico; Teresa and Melanie, who attended private schools; and Nicole, an adolescent who had been home tutored for a year after having been injured in a boating accident. The adolescents from the same regional high school immediately formed a clique, as did Teresa and Melanie. These subgroupings remained operative throughout the semester despite the leader's attempts to foster unity within the diversely composed group. Some differences of opinion emerged in developing a name for the members to use in referring to the group. After considerable discussion, Teresa and Melanie stated that they liked the name "No Dopes," whereas another subgroup preferred "Know Dopes." With the help of the leader a compromise was formed with "kNOw Dopes." Nevertheless, when the members considered printing the group name on T-shirts and possibly even selling bumper stickers, each clique wanted to do so with its own version of the group name.

The group focused on education about substance abuse and its consequences. The leader described the stages of substance use, misuse, abuse, and addiction (Beaudoin, 1991). The members then discussed instances of each in which they or people they knew had been involved in smoking marijuana. Melanie frequently referred to friends of hers who had smoked marijuana. In an orchestrated debate, some members insisted that substance use does not inevitably lead to addiction.

The leader promoted the development of self-control and assertiveness skills in avoiding the use of alcohol and other drugs. The members role played three situations in which the protagonists were at risk for acquiring drug abuse and other health problems. One situation involved Teresa and Melanie, who role played two friends who went out drinking. Afterward, Teresa offered Melanie some of her mother's pills for depression.

Another role-played situation involved Bob and Jerry, two adolescents who were enjoying themselves with magic tricks. Bob then asked Jerry to try some "sneezing powder," which turned out to be cocaine. A third situation was a "dare," in which Andres challenged another adolescent to shoot up a substance (heroin) without knowing what it was. In a variant of the third situation, the leader had Andres subsequently proposition Nicole for unprotected sexual activity, an event that turned out to be disruptive to the group. The following session of the group was largely devoted to discussions of social and sexual relationships. One session later the group was able to return to its consideration of drug abuse prevention.

The leader presented the members with a short list of potential guest speakers, including an attorney, a law enforcement official, and a former drug dealer who had spent 5 years in the state prison. The members rank ordered the potential speakers and rated the drug dealer first. Then the members took responsibility for contacting the guest speakers whom they were most interested in having come to the group. Completing the arrangements took several weeks. To the disappointment of the members, and the relief of parents who heard about it, the drug dealer could not speak because he had been rearrested! Guest speakers discussed public health topics. Jerry heckled a speaker who discussed the harmful consequences of drinking alcohol, an action that had him suspended from the group for the seventh session. Jerry required convincing by some of his friends in the group to return.

Another speaker brought along factual information about six possibly alcohol or drug-related deaths of adolescents that had occurred in the county in the past 2 years. Will told the members that Jonathan, his older brother, had a college roommate, Ted, who was badly injured in an auto accident. Ted went to a party on a Saturday night and the car he was in was hit by a drunk driver on the way back from the party. The other driver was killed. Will described how afterward Ted announced his homosexuality. Will wondered whether there was a connection between the events.

The members engaged in role-playing exercises that tested their resolve to avoid substance abuse. On the basis of a situation that he had been in recently, Bob played the part of an older adolescent who had asked him to come along to the river with some other teenagers to try some drugs. Bob actually seemed to have some mixed feelings about how to respond to the situation, which provoked merriment among the other members. In later sessions they teased him. "Hey Bob, have you done any fishing lately?"

In subsequent sessions, the members went on educational trips on which they learned about medical programs for helping substance abusers. After a visit to a substance abuse clinic, Elisha expressed interest in a career as an alcohol counselor. Although Nardia wanted to visit a cemetery to see the graves of teenagers who had died in alcohol-related events, the other members voted down the suggestion. Andres said it was "morbid."

During the last session the members indicated that of all the activities, they most enjoyed the field trips to treatment facilities. Three months later the group had a reunion at which Bob described how he drove a drunk friend home from a party and how his friend vomited in the rear seat of his parents' new Oldsmobile. Although his mother was unconcerned, his father was angry about what had happened to the car's appearance. Surprising to Bob, neither commented much about Bob's responsible behavior in taking care of his friend.

The leader felt that the group was a success in getting the adolescents to consider the issues of substance abuse. Nonetheless, he felt that the group would have worked better if he had a female coleader.

Some adults were in an uproar after hearing about some of the role-playing episodes and insisted that they would never allow their teenagers to attend such groups in the future. Nevertheless, additional groups were planned for the following year.

CONCLUSION

Mental disorders and substance abuse threaten the education, socialization, and well-being of many children and adolescents. Group work brings mental health and substance abuse care into school and community systems and is an important tool in maintaining and promoting the quality of life of children and adolescents. Group work is useful in maintaining youngsters' freedom from becoming dependent on addictive substances and increasing the chances that they will live constructive lives.

The preventive approach to group work is useful in helping youngsters maintain their mental health. The following chapter focuses on school performance as an important component of group work with children and adolescents.

Chapter 9

SCHOOL PERFORMANCE

SCHOOL PERFORMANCE
AS A SOCIAL PROBLEM

School performance comprises the interrelated areas of school attendance, academic performance, and achievement. Many factors contribute to school attendance, which is a prerequisite for participation and learning in school systems. For instance, runaway adolescents often discontinue attending school because they are fearful that their parents will find them at school (Rogers, Segal, & Graham, 1994). Furthermore, attendance has multiple effects. For example, it is an important factor in improving the low self-esteem and sense of loneliness experienced by many homeless children (Timberlake & Sabatino, 1994).

Pupil absenteeism is a term that sometimes is used to encompass truancy, or absenteeism from school without permission, along with school phobia or school refusal (Carroll, 1995). Absenteeism is a predictor of course failure and of dropping out of school (Gastright, 1989). Estimates of unexcused school absence range from 8% to 30% per day (Rodgers, 1980).

About one million students drop out of school annually (Campbell & Myrick, 1990). Overall, one out of four high school students drop out (Catterall, 1987) with the proportion reaching one out of two in the inner cities (Ranbom, 1986). Adolescents who drop out of high school have a higher unemployment rate, a lower median income, and are more likely to be incarcerated than those who graduate (Center for the Study of Social Policy, 1994; Kirsch, Jungeblut, Jenkins, & Kolstad, 1993).

Adolescents drop out of school due at least in part to a lack of fit between themselves and the school systems and a lack of support that they experience in the school.

Attendance is a necessary condition for academic performance and achievement (Coffee, 1981). Youngsters who are repeatedly suspended develop significant academic problems and are more likely to drop out of school (Dupper, 1994b). Academic performance involves carrying out learning activities, and achievement attests to persistence and success in learning. Achievement tests measure attainment of knowledge. Children and adolescents with positive attitudes toward school are more likely to obtain higher school grades and do well on standardized achievement tests (Myrick & Dixon, 1985).

Insufficient achievement is directly related to low levels of motivation. Early adolescence is often a period of decline in motivation and academic performance partly due to the transition from elementary to middle school (Eccles & Midgley, 1989). The difficulty in making the transition appears to be related at least in part to the greater emphasis on performance relative to tasks in middle school as compared to elementary school (Midgley, Anderman, & Hicks, 1995).

Furthermore, high rates of school mobility are related to poor academic performance (Felner, Primavera, & Cauce, 1981). For adolescents with a history of multiple school transfers, the transition to high school is related to lowered school performance and attendance. Providing social support through group work and reducing flux and complexity in school systems are important components in helping adolescent members cope with the transition to high school (Felner, Ginter, & Primavera, 1982).

Furthermore, academic performance and achievement are related to culture. Ethnic language skills may further social adaptation, upward mobility, and mainstream education of immigrant children and adolescents (Bankston & Zhou, 1995).

Indeed, language is a potent force in group work that has the potential to bind together persons from different countries, as with Spanish-speaking members from Central and South America, Mexico, the Caribbean, and Europe (Lopez, 1991). Group work with Latino (primarily Puerto Rican) children has shown the use of language to be emotionally laden (Bilides, 1992). Such group work indicates that Spanish is used to express identity, selectively form alliances within the group, and as a means for communicating covertly (Bilides, 1990).

Youngsters whose cultures are cooperative may have a difficult time in school systems with competitive norms. American and German schools lean toward being very competitive, Israeli schools have a cooperative basis with competitive aspects, and Polynesian schools that have become Westernized have become more competitive and less cooperative (Graves & Graves, 1978). An increase in competitiveness and a decrease in cooperativeness has been observed in secondary or middle school children as compared to primary or elementary school children in Japan (Shwalb, Shwalb, & Nakazawa, 1995). Jorge felt out of place in a school system in which he was one of the few children born in Mexico. Even when he enrolled in a group work program with three other children whose parents were born in Mexico, Jorge always felt that he should help and get along with other children and not show off his knowledge too much. Jorge was surprised to see that the other Mexican American children in the group were engaged in rivalries to see who could get better grades.

Ultimately, children and adolescents, as well as their families, sustain the consequences of school performance difficulties. Many children who are academically retained are at risk of developing social, emotional, and academic difficulties (Campbell & Bowman, 1993). Children and adolescents with low levels of academic performance and achievement have fewer life chances, including fewer occupational and economic opportunities, than higher-functioning youngsters.

PURPOSE OF GROUP WORK

The purpose of group work includes increasing school attendance, academic performance, and achievement. Group work uses motivational techniques and relies on peer processes to resolve the academic and social difficulties of children and adolescents. In school performance groups, the potential exists for members to receive social support and for the helpful factor of universality to emerge.

Group work is valuable to members and may increase the effectiveness of the school. An advantage of using group work to promote attendance is that it harnesses social influence to encourage members to come to school regularly. Given that attendance is a necessary precondition for the success of groups, it may appear to be paradoxical to use group work to improve attendance (Cimmarusti, James, Simpson, & Wright, 1984). Nevertheless, attendance and tardiness are suitable targets for intervention and prevention. Groups, which can be scheduled to meet at the beginning of the school day, can be designed to improve on operationally defined rates and levels of attendance and punctuality.

Given that attendance is required in schools and attending group work sessions also is expected, group work for improving attendance may be perceived by some members as a way of avoiding attending regular classes. Nevertheless, attending sessions on the subject of attending classes also is expected, as is attendance at school meetings, functions, and classes, which leaders communicate to members in the sessions. Through making the group classlike, emphasizing its relationship to the curriculum, and promoting good group attendance, attitudes favoring school performance are promoted.

Issues of academic performance and achievement readily lend themselves to group work in schools. Study skills can be practiced within supportive small groups (Schnedeker, 1991). Achievement can be recognized and encouraged. Efforts to positively influence achievement levels often are backed by school personnel, including teachers and pupil-personnel-service staff. Members readily grasp the appropriateness of working on achievement issues in school. Members who are uncomfortable with pressures for achievement in the classroom and school system may benefit from the solidarity of groups.

Peer tutoring in small groups has been shown to improve achievement among early and middle adolescents (Gyanani & Pahuja, 1995). In achievement groups that are composed of members of differing ages and academic skills, the process is akin to cross-age tutoring.

PROBLEM RECOGNITION
AND SOLUTION

Family (see Chapter 6), peer relationship and social competence (see Chapter 7), and mental health difficulties (see Chapter 8) may have an impact on school performance. For instance, Sally, an adolescent, was burned and disfigured in an accident involving a heating unit in her bedroom. After she was treated, she was reluctant to attend school, as she was afraid that the children would ridicule her appearance. Nevertheless, after her appearance improved sufficiently she was comfortably able to return to school.

Early childhood losses contribute to lowered academic performance and achievement (Fleisher, Berkovitz, Briones, Lovetro, & Morhar, 1987). Lorena was six when she lost her mother to breast cancer. She continued to live with her father and her two older sisters. There was a great deal of sorrow and stress in the home. Lorena's grades declined to the point where she was referred to an emotionally supportive school performance group.

Although the recognition of performance problems of children and adolescents is largely a function of school personnel, family members and community health care providers often are concerned and inquire about school performance. Screening of school performance takes place on both regular and exceptional bases.

The attendance and academic performances of potential dropouts are readily assessed and contribute to identifying youngsters with difficulties, providing them with timely help and contributing to their success in school (Dupper, 1994a). Early identification of potential dropouts, especially including children who fail first or second grade, is important for prevention (Praport, 1993). Formal assessments of achievement in academic areas, including reading, writing, spelling, and mathematics, regularly take place in schools, which are sites for the administration of standardized tests for placement in educational programs. When children or adolescents, their parents, and teachers observe problems related to academic performance, it is possible to enroll youngsters in group work.

A positive academic self-concept is directly related to achievement (Wiggins & Wiggins, 1992) and to later academic effort and persistence, educational aspirations, self-attributions for actions, high school graduation, and university attendance (Marsh, 1993). Academic performance leading to success at school is useful in promoting the positive academic self-concept of members. Academic performance becomes important to children as their academic self-concept develops and as they become conscious of their grade standing in comparison to their peers.

In addition to their academic self-concept, learning disabled, average, and gifted and talented members have physical and social self-concepts (Marsh, Chessor, Craven, & Roche, 1995). Damon was a fine basketball player and had many friends but performed below average in regard to grades. He had positive physical and social self-concepts, yet his academic self-concept was negative. As a member of a school performance group Damon learned to improve his academic performance and his academic self-concept.

For adolescents who are having academic difficulties, a series of events often leads to their leaving school. Developing a negative academic self-concept, having low expectations for school success, and having little motivation to improve study skills contribute to adolescents' risk of dropping out of school (Dupper, 1994a). Typical dropouts from low SES, underachieving, and minority backgrounds have high levels of social and sexual adjustment problems, concerns about physical health and appearance, and low levels of frustration tolerance (Charney, 1993). In contrast, atypical dropouts from middle SES backgrounds with a higher level of educational achievement based on standardized tests have noncohesive families and relatively high levels of drug use, depression, and educational difficulties as seen in low GPA's (Franklin & Streeter, 1992).

The awareness and identification of difficulties in attendance, academic performance, and achievement becomes pronounced when youngsters join groups. Beforehand, the attitude of many young children toward school attendance may be casual. Young children who come from families in which little emphasis is placed on academic performance and achievement may have little appreciation of its significance. Even more than for young children, for many adolescents the perception of school performance is at least in part a function of their participation in peer groups. Achievement is related to social acceptance (Glick, 1969). Low achieving adolescents in high school are more likely to be associated with peer groups beset with school performance problems (Downs & Rose, 1991; Rose & Downs, 1989).

Leaders are helpful in identifying the school performance problems of members. After members identify their difficulties they think of solutions. Leaders may encourage divergent thinking, producing many solutions, and developing a commitment to a limited yet feasible action plan (Easton, 1982). Objectives for members include (a) realizing that everyone has problems; (b) understanding the steps of problem-solving; (c) helping others find solutions; and (d) becoming aware of resources for problem solving within themselves, their families, and their peer groups.

The problem-solving abilities of members varies. Mildly handicapped adolescents, including those with learning disabilities, behavior disorders, or mild mental retardation, tend to be less able to solve social or interpersonal problems (Toro, 1984). Such members require greater help from leaders.

Members consider alternative means of solving identified problems. Whereas young children and early adolescents often have little understanding of this step, some older adolescents may understand it well (Moore, 1995). Selecting a strategy for problem solution involves decision making, including a consideration of potential consequences. For members who have difficulty with this step, leaders take an active role. Implementation of the strategy is carried out by the members and involves a strategy that can be set in motion during the group. The final step involves evaluating the effectiveness of the strategy, which may include changes in emotions or actions in situations as well as an improvement in attendance, study time, and grades.

PLANNING AND COMPOSITION

Leaders determine whether to plan to work with a group of youngsters who have one common set of problems or to plan a multiproblem group. In large schools and communities, it is often feasible to locate sufficient numbers of children or adolescents with one type of school performance problem and form a group solely with members with that type of problem (Rooney, 1977). Nevertheless, leaders must be wary of concentrating low-performing adolescents in each group, who may bond together and refrain from participating in regular school activities (Catterall, 1987).

In smaller schools and communities, fewer youngsters are usually available who have one type of problem, necessitating a combination of types within the group. In schools where youngsters have a combination of attendance, academic performance, and achievement difficulties it may be feasible to plan a combined group. An advantage is that by deemphasizing any one area of difficulty, it makes it more workable to form a supportive group.

After considering a range of school performance problems, leaders consider the type(s) to be focused on in the group. When attendance is to be addressed, children or adolescents who are truant, tardy, or who are in danger of dropping out of school are appropriate candidates for group work. In the early stages of planning school performance groups, leaders consult with school professionals in order to assess the achievement levels of youngsters as well as to obtain the interest, involvement, and support of the professionals (Rooney, 1977). Team staffings conducted at schools are likely to serve the planning process.

Leaders use their understanding of youngsters with academic performance and achievement difficulties in order to compose the group. One approach to composition is to form a group in which most or all members have substantial and comparable achievement difficulties, performing below grade level and below expectations for ability level. A potential limitation of such an approach is a lack of members with adequate or superior achievement levels, which would allow for adequate member-to-member instruction and demonstrations to boost the achievement level (Rooney, 1977). To deal with that limitation, a couple of alternatives for composing the group consist of including members with a range of academic abilities and achievement levels. In both alternatives, the group is composed as a microcosmic representative of a larger population of youngsters with diverse achievement levels, thereby allowing members to practice how to accommodate to those of different accomplishments as well as providing the opportunity to examine and increase their own levels of achievement (Easton, 1982).

In one alternative, to achieve a balance between members, pairs of high- and low-achievement youngsters are selected. If a great difference in school performance exists between the high and low achievers a tutoring arrangement is usually most appropriate. If the group is composed of varying ages and school abilities, cross-age tutoring may be feasible. Two hazards exist, for which leaders should take precautions, namely, the potential for the interaction to be limited to a mainly dyadic type and that of the group splitting into two distinct subunits based on levels of achievement. In another alternative, leaders compose the group with a majority of high achieving and a minority of low-achieving members. Such a compositional arrangement has two purposes. One purpose is to have many high-achieving members constructively demonstrate and promote the skill development of the few low-achieving members. A second purpose is to minimize potential undesirable effects of low-achieving children and adolescents on the school performance of high-achieving youngsters. In this compositional arrangement a majority (high achievers)-minority (low achievers) interaction pattern develops. A special consideration is that of a school performance group entirely composed of learning disabled youngsters, in which case there are high- and low-functioning members. The leaders compose a group in which each learning disabled member shares a school or learning problem with at least one and perhaps many members (West, Carlin, Baserman, & Milstein, 1978).

LEADERSHIP AND ACTIVITIES

In school performance groups in which members are able to help one another, leadership is a distributed function that stems from the leaders and the members. The functions of leadership include motivating the members to change. Coffee (1981) has developed a game that allows the leaders to focus the group on issues of motivation and attendance, including missing the bus, oversleeping, boredom, and helping at home.

Often, leadership style is directive and democratic. The leaders provide ideas for advancing the members' achievement levels. To promote achievement, leadership includes providing instruction related to learning and the acquisition of academic skills (Owen & Sabatino, 1989). In dropout prevention groups for adolescents, leadership is supportive without being excessively strict (Arons & Schwartz, 1993).

Leadership of groups for learning-disabled members involves speaking simply, allowing time for cognitive changes to occur, which depend on attitudinal shifts, and respecting changes in the members' family, peer, school, and community systems (Coche & Fisher, 1989). At least two models exist for providing leadership to learning-disabled children and adolescents: the authoritative figures model, which is most suitable for groups of hyperactive and behaviorally disabled members, and the orchestra leader model, which is most suitable for groups of less distractible members (Brown & Papagno, 1991). In the authoritative model, one leader, such as a teacher, is the authority figure who enforces rules of conduct and the other leader facilitates group interaction. In the orchestra model the leader is a conductor who gives cues to members when to speak. The leader also is responsible for giving warnings and sending disruptive members out of the room.

A primary leadership function is to demonstrate success in school performance, which can be accomplished through two means. One, the role of leaders is to function as models. Leaders may have experienced and overcome significant obstacles that affected their own school performance. Reducing the social distance between the leaders and the members and increasing the attractiveness of the leaders are likely to provide the bases for promoting change. Two, the leaders bring in and present children or adolescents who can demonstrate success at overcoming school performance problems. Youngsters who have been low achievers and then become higher achievers are worthwhile additions to the group in such a role. Such youngsters may be graduates of the school.

Leaders of school performance groups recognize that achievement is related to at least two types of goals (Urdan & Maehr, 1995). Learning or task goals, which are intrinsic, focus on improvement and mastery and often result in increased academic competence (Dweck & Leggett, 1988). Members with such goals tend to react well to challenges and when encountering difficulties tend to persevere and attempt to overcome obstacles (Butler, 1993). In contrast, performance or ability goals, which are extrinsic, represent concern with demonstrating ability and often are performed in order to appear competent in relation to other people (Newman & Schwager, 1995). Members with such goals are motivated to get good grades and finish assignments (Newman, 1991).

Achievement groups have some characteristics of task groups. Rooney (1977) has used task sheets in which members specify their academic problems, tasks, actions taken, and difficulties experienced.

In school performance groups, the leaders attend to the consequences of the difficulty and recognize efforts to reach the goal of improved performance. Leaders review actual progress of members in regard to the type of problem they experienced. For instance, when attendance is a concern it includes the number of days present and the number of days on time.

In groups in which most members have significant achievement problems the process includes a sequential and parallel set of leader-member interviews. If one takes play styles of children as an analogous situation, parallel solitary play represents a more basic stage of development than mutual, reciprocal play activity. Nevertheless, when an evenly distributed gradation of achievement levels exists, the heterogeneity adds vitality to the interaction.

In group work with primary-grade children, who either were recently grade retained or who were identified for retention, a program of eight sessions may be used (see Campbell & Bowman, 1993). The objectives of the first session are to clarify participants' expectations and build cohesiveness. The aim of the second session is to encourage members to explore their feelings, thoughts, and beliefs about their retention. The objectives of the third and fourth sessions are to teach members the concept of reframing and assist them in reframing some of their beliefs into more pleasant ones. The fifth session is oriented to looking at resources and successes of members, exploring what they can do well, helping them think of a time when through hard work they did better, and strengthen the belief that each member is capable and worthwhile. The objective of the sixth session is to use creative dramatics to help members learn ways to cope with challenges that may confront them in being retained. The seventh session is devoted to exploring role-played examples of children doing their school work and to showing members that they can apply what they have learned in the group to their own school work. The purpose of the eighth session is to end the group with an enjoyable motivational activity that develops their interest in making a fresh start in school.

In an example of group work with undermotivated middle-grade children, the first session, "Getting Started," consists of members sharing personal interests (see Campbell & Myrick, 1990). Members participate in a guided fantasy in which they think about the school as a pleasant place. Then, they discuss and list actions related to school success on a chalkboard. In the second session, "Who's in Control?" members focus on being responsible and honest to themselves. They categorize, read aloud, and discuss a list of statements pertaining to taking responsibility for self and placing responsibility on others. Through role playing, members further study the meaning of responsibility. In the third session, "Assuming Responsibility," members explore popular phrases often used by adolescents to shirk responsibility. Then, members talk about phrases they use and develop ways of restating such phrases. Finally, members role play situations that involve taking responsibility. In the fourth session, "The Positive Self," members discuss ideas related to self-concept and accept compliments and encouragement. Members develop ways to develop positive statements and habits. Leaders encourage members to imagine themselves doing homework, finding answers to study questions, and asking for help. In session five, "Plan for Success," members attend to short-term and long-term goals.

Leaders pair the members in supportive buddy systems. Members develop plans for improving school performance and contract with their buddies to commit to a plan of action. In the sixth (last) session, "The Encouragement Card," members help each other identify personal strengths. They brainstorm a list of traits and exchange positive feedback. Members are encouraged to say affirmations recorded on cards throughout the day.

In some groups, such as those for educable mentally handicapped adolescents in high school, pregroup sessions are used to determine membership and to help members differentiate between group work and their classes (Baumhardt & Lawrence, 1983). The initial pregroup session includes an explanation of group work and what to expect in the group. Leaders establish group rules pertaining to maintaining confidentiality, banning physical violence, and prohibiting verbal interruptions with the consequence for rule violation consisting of the rule breaker leaving the room for the remainder of the session. In an opening exercise, leaders ask members to identify one thing they liked and one thing they disliked about school.

In the beginning phase of school performance groups, the sessions involve making introductions and establishing cohesive relationships.

To improve their chances of success, leaders should clearly specify the purposes of school performance groups, for example, improving attendance, grades, or learning (Gitterman, 1979).

In the middle phase, groups work on an elaboration of the problem-solving scheme. For instance, in a group for fifth- and sixth-grade children, the leader asked the members to anonymously write down a problem (Myrick & Dixon, 1985). The written statements were collected and with the permission of the members one was read aloud. The leader asked the members a series of three discussion questions, namely, how they would feel if they had a problem such as the one read, how they would act if they had such feelings, and what someone could do in such a situation.

Leaders identify attendance, academic performance, and achievement obstacles to be overcome. In structured short-term groups used to promote academic performance and prevent dropouts in intermediate or middle schools, weekly goals are set and monitored (Blum & Jones, 1993). The objectives of the first session include getting acquainted, learning expectations, and acknowledging all members' strengths. The objectives of the second session include sharing the week's goals and accomplishments, helping each other, analyzing individual study habits, and reviewing and completing a goal-setting sheet. The objectives of the third and fourth sessions include discussing progress with study skills and study habits and discussing self-confidence. The objectives of the fifth session include learning how to communicate using "I Messages." The objectives of the sixth session include reporting on recorded attendance and academic performance. The objectives of the seventh session include describing interpersonal skills used and learning to use the problem-solving model through role playing actual problems identified by members. The objectives of the eighth session include listing and reciting one or more positive characteristics of members, accepting compliments, and completing an evaluation. The objectives of the ninth (follow-up) session include receiving evaluations from the leader, congratulating each other, and planning monthly meetings to maintain progress.

In groups designed to promote achievement among male intermediate school students, discussion questions include What is achievement? How do you achieve? How do you not achieve? What is responsibility?

What do you want to be in 5 years (i.e., what goals do you have)? What do you like about school? What do you dislike about school? What will you like about your future job? What will you like least about your future job? (Balsanek, 1986). In the ending phase, the members identify their accomplishments and leaders make arrangements for monitoring and maintaining improvements in school performance.

AN EXAMPLE: THE BOOK HITTERS

According to an internal report prepared by the education department of a large western state, fewer than half of high school students in the central area of one of the largest cities in the state were graduated in the past year. The pupil personnel staff at a high school with a particularly high dropout rate were particularly concerned about the academic performance of many of the 11th-grade students, few of whom appeared to be taking the steps necessary for graduating from high school. Whereas some staff members offered some individualized help for such difficulties on a sporadic basis, most felt that another approach should be tried. At a meeting about the academic problems of students, staff members considered potential intervention approaches and discussed the idea of forming a group. After some initial discussion, the principal approved the idea of group work and suggested that a staff member present a proposal at an upcoming community board meeting.

The meeting, which was held the following month, had some difficult moments for the staff member, who thought at times that the proposal would not pass. Three board members expressed their concern that children in a school performance group would be identified as having academic difficulties, which would tarnish their academic reputations and chances for school success. A parent who attended the meeting shouted that the children would be labeled as "dummies" and "failures." The staff member calmly indicated that the purpose of the group was to help children who were already having difficulties so that they would succeed. After describing working principles, confidentiality, and activities, the community board gave their approval with a 5 to 4 vote.

Group work was designed to help adolescents who were identified by the pupil personnel services team as being at significant risk for dropping out of school. Usually, such adolescents were failing two or more academic subjects in the current school year. The team members discussed group work with teachers and made requests for referrals. Within 2 weeks the pupil personnel staff received 16 referrals of adolescents in academic distress from four high school teachers.

After screening the referrals and reviewing attendance and grade records, the pupil personnel team interviewed each potential member. Whereas most of the interviewed adolescents were deemed eligible according to the established criteria, two adolescents were deemed low risk. One other adolescent became seriously physically ill due to complications stemming from appendicitis. Of the 13 remaining adolescents, 9 appeared suitable for participating and expressed their willingness to join the group.

The group met at an isolated club room. Two members required directions to find the room within the school. It was comfortably furnished and, owing to its color scheme, the members called it "the blue room." It was adjacent to a kitchen and a large recreation hall that housed a piano.

The first two sessions consisted of an orientation to and discussion of the purpose of the group. Despite agreeing to participate in the group, some of the adolescents began with an attitude that one member expressed as, "I don't need to be in here!" To counter some members' discomfort about the group's stated purpose of helping them succeed at school, the leaders conducted an exercise in which the members described their achievements at school. The members were pleased to think of the group as a club. Indeed, many of them were excited to work on a newsletter and go on trips that would take them out of school. After the members learned of others who benefited from such a group, the leaders discerned greater acceptance from the members. The leaders emphasized the more constructive meaning of "The Book Hitters," the group name that was enthusiastically endorsed by the members, and deemphasized the allusions to violence inherent in the other meaning.

The third and fourth sessions involved a discussion of careers. Many of the members had little idea of what the term meant or how to apply it to their own lives. "What's a career?" Francesca asked. "How about shooting up forever?" Nardia answered.

The leaders realized that the members had to change their view of their ultimate chances for employment to realize that they could work. They affirmed the value of each member and provided them with examples of other high school students who had succeeded in their careers.

The leaders asked the members to identify several occupational possibilities for themselves. Members replied as follows: doctor, nurse, EMT (emergency medical technician), undertaker, police officer, and cook. "You're never going to become no doctor," Nardia said. To the chagrin of the leaders the rest of the group laughed. At the suggestion of one of the leaders, several members gathered career information from the public library, which was a new experience for some of them.

"Where's the library?" Nicole asked. Nevertheless, it became apparent that much of the career material the members had gathered from the library was antiquated. Some of the members laughed at some of the pictures they saw in the books. "Did people really dress like that then?" Monica asked. Francesca added, "Look at that hair!" Then, the members decided to find professionals who were willing to speak to the group about the educational requirements for various careers. The leaders used the resources of the pupil personnel services team to reach such people and gain their participation in later sessions of the group. The members invited an insurance agent to come to the group. He surprised many of them by attempting to sell life insurance policies to their parents.

In the fifth and sixth sessions, the leader helped members identify resources that promoted their success at school as well as problems that they felt interfered with it. The members soon began complaining about unsympathetic teachers and the leaders attempted to modify members' expectations of teachers. Although the members thought there was little to do about crumbling buildings, leaky roofs, and having classes in closets, they did brainstorm a number of strategies, including informing the janitor, calling the newspaper, and raising money for schools.

Conflict with peers and violence were discussed from a problem-solving perspective. Ultimately, many members thought it best to avoid violence. "Stay away from those troublemakers," said Anne. "Like you," said Nardia. By this time the members had grown accustomed to

Nardia's comments, although the leaders thought she should speak differently. The objective of the seventh and eighth sessions was the challenge of making the school a more rewarding experience for the members. The group brainstormed many ideas, including having teacher and student appreciation days, and honoring all students for their abilities and accomplishments in school. Nardia said, "If you honor everyone, it's like honoring no one." Several members nodded their heads in agreement. The members invited the principal to come to the school and presented her with their ideas and a birthday cake. To the members' surprise, she liked and praised the members' ideas and called on the group to put them into effect.

The group circulated fliers announcing the appreciation days. However, the fliers appeared to be taken down almost as soon as they were put up. When one of the leaders spotted Nardia taking them down she confronted her. Tearfully, the girl admitted to doing it. The leaders arranged for some individual sessions for Nardia with the school guidance counselor. Nardia said that she no longer wanted to be in the group and the leaders complied with her request. Her leaving the group caused a temporary crisis, but the group continued to meet.

The members called for nominees and received several names. They decided to give all the nominees awards. The members raised money from the parents' organization for ceremonies honoring the teachers and students. Fund-raising turned out to be more challenging for some of the members than they had anticipated.

Yet, many of the remaining members put in substantial amounts of time on the project. The leaders warned them not to neglect their studies! The 9th through 12th sessions were devoted to improving members' study skills. The leader detected a lack of motivation among some members. "Why study? All I get is lousy grades," said Nathalie. Members discussed the pros and cons of using the study hall. Three members tried it and two found it actually helped them. Paul said it was a great place to meet girls.

Some members explored working together to help each other with assignments. The leaders had tried to match the members on the basis of budding school interests but after some personality clashes realized that it would be better for the members to pair up themselves.

Following a suggestion from a supervisory member of the pupil personnel services team, the leaders brought in printed material to help members learn to follow instructions on exams and homework. The members practiced reviewing their work, giving and accepting positive and negative feedback, and establishing their own standards for performance. The leaders unsuccessfully attempted to refrain from providing feedback. Members worked on actual homework assignments and monitored their grades.

The members role played communicating with parents about doing homework. Most of them particularly relished the role of being parents who nagged their children to complete their homework. Paul and Nicole said they spent too much time on homework. Nevertheless, when the leader found out how much time they actually spent, they revised some of their notions.

For the 13th and 14th sessions, which were the ending ones, the leader invited the teachers and members of the pupil personnel services team, including the guidance counselor, to discuss the school as a learning environment. The members seemed lost by the discussion. When the members discussed who was responsible for school performance, to the leader's surprise, only four members attributed their school success to the effort they put in to their learning. It was difficult for the leaders to determine whether the members were serious in pointing to others as causes for any success they had at school. Whereas the leaders were somewhat astonished to hear such comments at the end of the group, most of the remaining members were passing more subjects, although one member was doing worse. The dropout rate of the members as a group turned out to be lower than that of the other 11th-grade students and lower than that of those students who had been invited to come but did not attend.

Better relationships were formed between the members and their teachers. The leaders were amazed at the change in attitude of most members toward their teachers. Indeed, it was very enlightening for the members to hear about some of the outstanding accomplishments of teachers in their school.

The principal was convinced that the group was a success and that it should be continued the following year. Members whose grades improved graduated from the group whereas the others were invited to participate in an additional group of the same type their senior year. Three accepted the invitation.

CONCLUSION

School performance groups often have the full cooperation of family and community members. Occasionally, however, family and community members may object to the stated purpose of raising academic performance and achievement levels. Some of the concerns may be in regard to an implicit message that their children have been underperforming in school. Furthermore, some may perceive the group as a social control mechanism. Leaders who work with parents and community members may address such concerns and increase their motivation by presenting the group in a positive manner.

Group work can improve school performance through maintaining attendance, reducing truancy and dropping out, and improving the academic functioning and achievement of members. By carefully selecting members, understanding the goals of members, and being aware of the factors that influence school performance, leaders may effectively help children and adolescents.

REFERENCES

Achenbach, T. M. (1982). *Developmental psychopathology* (2nd ed.). New York: John Wiley.

Admunson-Beckmann, K., & Lucas, A. R. (1989). Gaining a foothold in the aftermath of divorce. *Social Work in Education, 12,* 5-15.

Alden, S. E., Pettigrew, L. E., & Skiba, E. A. (1970). The effect of individual-contingent group reinforcement on popularity. *Child Development, 41,* 1191-1196.

Alpert-Gillis, L. J., Pedro-Carroll, J. L., & Cowen, E. L. (1989). The Children of Divorce Intervention Program: Development, implementation, and evaluation of a program for young urban children. *Journal of Consulting and Clinical Psychology, 57,* 583-589.

American Psychiatric Association. (1994). *Diagnostic and statistical manual of mental disorders* (4th ed.). Washington, DC: Author.

Anderson, R. F., Kinney, J., & Gerler, E. R. (1984). The effects of divorce groups on children's classroom behavior and attitudes toward divorce. *Elementary School Guidance & Counseling, 19,* 70-76.

Anesko, K. M., Scholock, G., Ramirez, R., & Levine, F. M. (1987). The Homework Problem Checklist: Assessing children's homework difficulties. *Behavioral Assessment, 9,* 179-185.

Armstrong, J. H. (1978). The effect of group counseling on the self-concept, academic performance, and reading level of a selected group of high school students (Doctoral dissertation, Wayne State University, 1978). *Dissertation Abstracts International, 40,* 1332-A.

Arons, R. D., & Schwartz, F. S. (1993). Interdisciplinary coleadership of high school groups for dropout prevention: Practice issues. *Social Work, 38,* 9-14.

Ashby, M. R., Gilchrist, L. D., & Miramontez, A. (1987). Group treatment for sexually abused American Indian adolescents. *Social Work With Groups, 10,* 21-32.

Balsanek, J. A. (1986). Group intervention for underachievers in the intermediate school. *Social Work in Education, 9,* 26-32.

Bandura, A. (1977). Self-efficacy: Toward a unifying theory of behavioral change. *Psychological Review, 84,* 191-215.

Bankston, C. L., III, & Zhou, M. (1995). Effects of minority-language literacy on the academic achievement of Vietnamese youths in New Orleans. *Sociology of Education, 68,* 1-17.

Barclay, J. (1966). Sociometry: Rationale and technique for effecting behavior change in the elementary school. *Personnel and Guidance Journal, 45,* 1067-1075.

Baumhardt, L. A., & Lawrence, S. (1983). Transforming negatively labeled student groups into support groups. *Social Work in Education, 5,* 229-240.

Beare, P. L. (1991). Philosophy, instructional methodology, training, and goals of teachers of the behaviorally disordered. *Behavioral Disorders, 16,* 211-218.

Beaudoin, E. (1991). Assessment and intervention with chemically dependent students. *Social Work in Education, 13,* 78-89.

Berkovitz, I. H. (1975). Indications for use of groups in secondary schools and review of literature. In I. H. Berkovitz (Ed.), *When schools care: Creative use of groups in secondary schools* (pp. 26-40). New York: Brunner/Mazel.

Berkovitz, I. H. (1987a). Application of group therapy in secondary schools. In F. J. C. Azima & L. H. Richmond (Eds.), *Adolescent group psychotherapy* (pp. 99-123). Madison, CT: International Universities Press.

Berkovitz, I. H. (1987b). Value of group counseling in secondary schools. *Adolescent Psychiatry, 14,* 522-545.

Berkovitz, I. H. (1989). Application of group therapy in secondary schools. In F. J. Cramer & L. H. Richmond (Eds.), *Adolescent group psychotherapy* (pp. 99-123). Madison, CT: International Universities Press.

Bertcher, H. J., & Maple, F. (1985). Elements and issues in group composition. In M. Sundel, P. Glasser, R. Sarri, & R. Vinter (Eds.), *Individual change through small groups* (2nd ed., pp. 180-202). New York: Free Press.

Bilides, D. G. (1990). Race, color, ethnicity, and class: Issues of biculturalism in school-based adolescent counseling groups. *Social Work With Groups, 13,* 43-58.

Bilides, D. G. (1992). Reaching inner-city children: A group work program model for a public middle school. *Social Work With Groups, 15,* 129-144.

Birelson, P. (1981). The validity of depression disorders in childhood and the development of a self-rating scale: A research report. *Journal of Child Psychology and Psychiatry, 22,* 73-88.

Birmingham, M. S. (1986). An out-patient treatment programme for adolescent substance abusers. *Journal of Adolescence, 9,* 123-133.

Blau, B., & Rafferty, J. (1970). Changes in friendship status as a function of reinforcement. *Child Development, 41,* 113-121.

Blum, D. J., & Jones, L. A. (1993). Academic growth group and mentoring program for potential dropouts. *The School Counselor, 40,* 207-217.

Bogdaniak, R. C., & Piercy, F. P. (1987). Therapeutic issues of adolescent children of alcoholics (AdCA) groups. *International Journal of Group Psychotherapy, 37,* 569-588.

Bok, M. (1980). External versus internal evaluation. *Social Work in Education, 2,* 9-19.

Boren, R. (1983, June). The therapeutic effects of a school-based intervention program for children of the divorced. *Dissertation Abstracts International, 43*(12), 3811-A-3812-A.

Bornstein, M. T., Bornstein, P. H., & Walters, H. A. (1988). Children of divorce: Empirical evaluation of a group-treatment program. *Journal of Clinical Child Psychology, 17,* 248-254.

Borrine, M., Handal, P., Brown, N., & Searight, H. (1991). Family conflict and adolescent adjustment in intact, divorced, and blended families. *Journal of Consulting and Clinical Psychology, 59,* 753-755.

Bowker, M. A. (1982). Children and divorce: Being in between. *Elementary School Guidance and Counseling, 17,* 126-130.

Breidenbach, D. C. (1984). Behavioral skills training for students: A preventive program. *Social Work in Education, 6,* 231-240.

Brown, C. D., & Papagno, N. I. (1991). Structured group therapy for learning and behaviorally disabled children and adolescents. *Journal of Child and Adolescent Group Therapy, 1,* 43-57.

Brown, J., Haas, R., & Portes, P. (1991). Identifying family factors that predict children's adjustment to divorce. *Journal of Divorce and Remarriage, 15,* 87-101.

Brown, J., & Swanson, A. (1988). Reemergent trends in school social work practice. *Social Work in Education, 10,* 88-95.

Brown, W., & Kingsley, R. F. (1975). The effect of individual contracting and guided group interaction upon behavior disordered youth's self-concept. *The Journal of School Health, 45,* 399-401.

Burnett, M., & Newcomer, L. (1990). Group counseling children of divorce. *Journal of Divorce, 13,* 69-77.

Butler, R. (1993). Effects of task- and ego-achievement goals on information seeking during task engagement. *Journal of Personality and Social Psychology, 65,* 18-31.

Campbell, C., & Bowman, R. P. (1993). The "fresh start" support club: Small-group counseling for academically retained children. *Elementary School Guidance and Counseling, 27,* 172-185.

Campbell, C. A., & Myrick, R. D. (1990). Motivational group counseling for low-performing students. *The Journal for Specialists in Group Work, 15,* 43-50.

Carll, E. K. (1994). Disaster intervention with children and families: National and state initiatives. *The Child, Youth, and Family Services Quarterly, 17,* 21-23.

Carlson, C., Paavola, J., & Talley, R. (1995). Historical, current, and future models of schools as health care delivery settings. *School Psychology Quarterly, 10,* 184-202.

Carnegie Task Force on Education of Young Adolescents (1989). *Turning points: Preparing American youth for the 21st century.* New York: Carnegie Council on Adolescent Development of the Carnegie Corporation.

Carroll, H. C. M. (1995). Pupil absenteeism: A Northern European perspective. *School Psychology International, 16,* 227-247.

Carroll, M. (1980). School practice and the mental health needs of pupils. *Social Work in Education, 2,* 12-28.

Catterall, J. S. (1987). An intensive group counseling dropout prevention intervention: Some cautions on isolating at-risk adolescents within high schools. *American Educational Research Journal, 24,* 521-540.

Cebollero, A., Cruise, K., & Stollak, G. (1987). The long term effects of divorce. *Journal of Divorce, 10,* 219-227.

Center for the Study of Social Policy (1994). *Kids count data book: State profiles of child well-being.* Washington, DC: Author.

Chandler, M. J. (1976). Social cognition: A selective review of current research. In W. F. Overton & J. M. Gallagher (Eds.), *Knowledge and development* (Vol. 1, pp. 93-147). New York: Plenum.

Charney, H. (1993). Project Achievement: A six-year study of a dropout prevention program in bilingual schools. *Social Work in Education, 15,* 113-117.

Christian, A. A., Henderson, J., Morse, B. A., & Wilson, N. C. (1983). A family-focused treatment program for emotionally disturbed students. *Social Work in Education, 5,* 165-177.

Cimmarusti, R. A., James, M. C., Simpson, D. W., & Wright, C. E. (1984). Treating the context of truancy. *Social Work in Education, 6,* 201-211.

Clarke, G., & Lewinsohn, P. M. (1989). The coping with depression course: A group psychoeducational intervention for unipolar depression. *Behaviour Change, 6,* 54-69.

Coche, J. M., & Fisher, J. H. (1989). Group psychotherapy with learning disabled adolescents. In F. J. C. Azima & L. H. Richmond (Eds.), *Adolescent group psychotherapy* (pp. 125- 142). Madison, CT: International Universities Press Inc.

Coffee, C. L. (1981). Group work and the school attendance game. *School Social Work Journal, 5,* 79-81.

Coffman, S. G. (1988). Conflict-resolution strategy for adolescents with divorced parents. *The School Counselor, 36,* 61-66.

Cohen, B. (Ed.). (1967). *Guidelines for future research on group counseling in the public school setting.* Washington, DC: American Personnel and Guidance Association.

Cole, D., & Kammer, P. P. (1984). Support groups for children of divorced parents. *Elementary School Guidance & Counseling, 19,* 88-94.

Congress, E. P., & Lynn, M. (1994). Group work programs in public schools: Ethical dilemmas and cultural diversity. *Social Work in Education, 16,* 107-114.

Corcoran, K., & Fischer, J. (1987). *Measures for clinical practice: A sourcebook.* New York: Free Press.

Cordell, A. S., & Bergman-Meador, B. (1991). The use of drawings in group intervention for children of divorce. *Journal of Divorce & Remarriage, 17,* 139-155.

Coward, R. T., & Rose, S. R. (1982). Coming of age in contemporary rural environments. *Child, Youth, and Family Services Quarterly, 5,* 3-5.

Cowen, E. L., Hightower, A. D., Pedro-Carroll, J., & Work, W. C. (1989). School-based models for primary prevention programming with children. *Prevention in Human Services, 7,* 133-160.

Cowen, E. L., Pederson, A., Babigian, H., Izzo, L. D., & Trost, M. A. (1973). Long-term follow-up of early detected vulnerable children. *Journal of Consulting & Clinical Psychology, 41,* 438-446.

Cox, K. L., & Price, K. (1990). Breaking through: Incident drawings with adolescent substance abusers. *The Arts in Psychotherapy, 17,* 333-337.

Crosbie-Burnett, M., & Newcomer, L. L. (1990). Group counseling children of divorce: The effects of a multimodal intervention. *Journal of Divorce, 13,* 69-78.

Curran, D. K. (1987). *Adolescent suicidal behavior.* Washington, DC: Hemisphere Publishing.

Cutsinger, C. J., & Glick, A. (1983). Structured group treatment model for latency-age children of divorce. *School Social Work Journal, 8,* 16-27.

Daratha, B. M. (1992). Behavior impaired students: Putting them on the right track. *Schools in the Middle, 2,* 19-22.

Darrow, N. R., & Lynch, M. T. (1983). The use of photography activities with adolescent groups. *Social Work With Groups, 6,* 77-83.

de Anda, D. (1985). Structured vs. nonstructured groups in the teaching of problem solving. *Social Work in Education, 7,* 80-89.

Deluty, R. H. (1979). Children's Action Tendency Scale: A self-reported measure of aggressiveness, assertiveness, and submissiveness in children. *Journal of Consulting and Clinical Psychology, 47,* 1061-1071.

Dewey, J. (1933). *How we think.* Boston: Heath.

Downs, W. R., & Rose, S. R. (1991). The relationship of adolescent peer groups to the incidence of psychosocial problems. *Adolescence, 26,* 473-492.

Dunnington, M. J. (1957). Behavioral differences of sociometric status groups in a nursery school. *Child Development, 28,* 103-111.

Dupper, D. R. (1994a). Preventing school dropouts: Guidelines for school social work practice. *Social Work in Education, 15,* 141-149.

Dupper, D. R. (1994b). Reducing out-of-school suspensions: A survey of attitudes and barriers. *Social Work in Education, 16,* 115-123.

Dweck, C. S., & Leggett, E. L. (1988). A social-cognitive approach to motivation and personality. *Psychological Review, 95,* 256-273.

Easton, F. (1982). Using peer-group discussion in the mainstreaming of handicapped pupils. *Social Work in Education, 4,* 16-25.

Eccles, J. S., & Midgley, C. (1989). Stage/environment fit: Developmentally appropriate classrooms for early adolescents. In R. E. Ames & C. Ames (Eds.), *Research on motivation in education* (Vol. 3, pp. 139-186). New York: Academic Press.

Edleson, J. L., & Rose, S. D. (1978, November). *A behavioral roleplay test for assessing children's social skills.* Paper presented at the 12th annual meeting of the Association for the Advancement of Behavior Therapy, Chicago.

Effron, A. K. (1980). Children and divorce: Help from an elementary school. *Social Casework, 61,* 305-312.

Elardo, P., & Cooper, M. (1977). *AWARE: Activities for social development.* Reading, MA: Addison-Wesley.

Elias, M. J., Gara, M., & Ubriaco, M. (1985). Sources of stress and coping in children's transition to middle school: An empirical analysis. *Journal of Clinical Child Psychology, 14,* 112-118.

Elias, M. J., Gara, M., Ubriaco, M., Rothbaum, P. A., Clabby, J. F., & Schuyler, T. (1986). Impact of a preventive social problem solving intervention on children's coping with middle-school stressors. *American Journal of Community Psychology, 14,* 259-275.

Eliot, A. O. (1990). Group coleadership: A new role for parents of adolescents with anorexia and bulimia nervosa. *International Journal of Group Psychotherapy, 40,* 339-351.

Emery, R. E. (1988). *Marriage, divorce, and children's adjustment.* Newbury Park, CA: Sage.

Epstein, Y. M., Borduin, C. M., & Wexler, A. S. (1985). The Children Helping Children Program: A case illustration. *Special Services in the Schools, 2,* 73-93.

Eth, S., & Pynoos, R. (1985). Developmental perspective on psychic trauma in childhood. In C. R. Figley (Ed.), *Trauma and its wake: Vol. 1. The study and treatment of post-traumatic stress disorder.* New York: Brunner/Mazel.

Evans, A., & Neel, J. (1980). School behaviors of children from one-parent and two-parent homes. *Principal, 60,* 38-39.

Farmer, S., & Galaris, D. (1993). Support groups for children of divorce. *The American Journal of Family Therapy, 21,* 40-50.

Fatout, M., & Rose, S. R. (1995). *Task groups in the social services.* Thousand Oaks, CA: Sage.

Fauber, F., Long, N., & McCombs, A. (1988). Early adolescent adjustment to recent parental divorce. *Journal of Consulting and Clinical Psychology, 56,* 624-626.

Felner, R. D., Farber, S., & Primavera, J. (1983). Transitions and stressful life events: A model for primary prevention. In R. D. Felner, L. Jason, J. Moritsugu, & S. Farber (Eds.), *Prevention psychology: Theory, research, and practice.* Elmsford, NY: Pergamon.

Felner, R. D., Ginter, M., & Primavera, J. (1982). Primary prevention during school transitions: Social support and environmental structure. *American Journal of Community Psychology, 10,* 277-290.

Felner, R. D., Primavera, J., & Cauce, A. M. (1981). The impact of school transitions: A focus for preventive efforts. *American Journal of Community Psychology, 9,* 449-459.

Fine, S., Forth, A., Gilbert, M., & Haley, G. (1991). Group therapy for adolescent depressive disorder: A comparison of social skills and therapeutic support. *Journal of American Academy of Child and Adolescent Psychiatry, 30,* 79-85.

Fischer, J. & Corcoran, K. (1994). *Measures for clinical practice: A sourcebook: Vol. 1. Couples, families, and children* (2nd ed.). New York: Free Press.

Fisher, H. A. (1989). Magic circle: Group therapy for children. *Social Work in Education, 11,* 260-265.

Fleisher, S. J., Berkovitz, I. H., Briones, L., Lovetro, K., & Morhar, N. (1987). Antisocial behavior, school performance, and reactions to loss: The value of group counseling and communication skills training. *Adolescent Psychiatry, 14,* 546-555.

Forehand, R., Thomas, A. M., Wierson, M., Brody, G., & Fauber, R. (1990). Role of maternal functioning and parenting skills in adolescent functioning following parental divorce. *Journal of Abnormal Psychology, 99,* 278-283.

Franklin, C., & Streeter, C. L. (1992). Differential characteristics of high-achieving/high-income and low- achieving/low-income dropout youths: Considerations for treatment programs. *Social Work in Education, 14,* 42-55.

Franzoi, S. L., Davis, M. H., & Vasquez-Suson, K. A. (1994). Two social worlds: Social correlates and stability of adolescent status groups. *Journal of Personality and Social Psychology, 67,* 462-473.

Freeman, E. M. (1985). Analyzing the organizational context of schools. *Social Work in Education, 7,* 141-159.

Fujii, M. (1989). School social work with groups: A cognitive-developmental approach. *School Social Work Journal, 13,* 18-25.

Furman, L. (1990). Video therapy: An alternative for the treatment of adolescents. *The Arts in Psychotherapy, 17,* 165-169.

Gallagher, K. (1983). Improving coping in an adolescent population. (Doctoral Dissertation, Ferkauf Graduate School, Yeshiva University, 1983). *Dissertation Abstracts International, 43.*

Gardner, R. A. (1970). *The boys and girls book about divorce.* New York: Bantam Books.

Garvin, C. D. (1977). Strategies for group work with adolescents. In W. J. Reid & L. Epstein (Eds.), *Task-centered practice* (pp. 157-167). New York: Columbia University Press.

Garvin, V., Leber, D., & Kalter, N. (1991). Children of divorce: Predictors of change following preventive intervention. *American Journal of Orthopsychiatry, 61,* 438-447.

Gastright, J. F. (1989). Don't base your dropout program on somebody else's problem. *Research Bulletin, 4,* 1-4.

Germain, C. B. (1988). School as a living environment within the community. *Social Work in Education, 10,* 260-276.

Gitterman, N. P. (1979). Group services for learning disabled children and their parents. *Social Casework, 60,* 217-226.

Glasgow, G. F., & Gouse-Sheese, J. (1995). Themes of rejection and abandonment in group work with Caribbean adolescents. *Social Work With Groups, 17,* 3-27.

Glassman, V., & Reid, M. (1985). Services to children and families undergoing separation and divorce. *Social Work in Education, 8,* 66-69.

Glick, O. (1969). Person-group relationships and the effect of group properties on academic achievement in the elementary school classroom. *Psychology in the Schools, 6,* 197-203.

Gliksman, L., Smythe, P. C., Gorman, J., & Rush, B. (1980). The adolescent alcohol questionnaire: Its development and psychometric evaluation. *Journal of Drug Education, 10,* 209-227.

Goldstein, A. P., Heller, K., & Sechrest, L. B. (1966). *Psychotherapy and the psychology of behavior change.* New York: John Wiley.

Golner, J. H. (1983). Mental health intervention in the schools. *Social Work in Education, 6,* 15-31.

Graver, C. (1987). Group counseling program helps students deal with divorce. *NASSP (National Association of Secondary School Principals) Bulletin, 71,* 32-34.

Graves, N. B., & Graves, T. D. (1978). The impact of modernization on the personality of a Polynesian people. *Human Organization, 37,* 115-135.

Grych, J. H., & Fincham, F. D. (1992). Interventions for children of divorce: Toward greater integration of research and action. *Psychological Bulletin, 111,* 434-454.

Guggenbuhl, A. (1991). Tales and fiction: Group psychotherapy for children and juveniles at the children and educational counseling centre of the state of Bern. *School Psychology International, 12,* 7-16.

Guidubaldi, J., Cleminshaw, H. W., Perry, J. D., & McLaughlin, C. S. (1983). The impact of parental divorce on children: Report of the nationwide NASP study. *School Psychology Review, 12,* 300-323.

Gump, P. V., & Sutton-Smith. (1955). Activity setting and social interaction: A field study. *American Journal of Orthopsychiatry, 25,* 755-760.

Gwynn, C. A., & Brantley, H. T. (1987). Effects of a divorce group intervention for elementary school children. *Psychology in the Schools, 24,* 161-164.

Gyanani, T. C., & Pahuja, P. (1995). Effects of peer tutoring on abilities and achievement. *Contemporary Educational Psychology, 20,* 469-475.

Hage, J., & Aiken, M. (1980). Program change and organizational properties. In H. Resnick & R. J. Patti (Eds.), *Change from within: Humanizing social welfare organizations* (pp. 157-171). Philadelphia: Temple University Press.

Hanson, G., & Liber, G. (1989). A model for the treatment of adolescent children of alcoholics. *Alcoholism Treatment Quarterly, 6,* 53-69.

Harper, K. V., & Shillito, L. S. (1991). Group work with bulimic adolescent females in suburbia. *Social Work With Groups, 14,* 43-56.

Hartup, W. W. (1970). Peer interaction and social organization. In P. H. Mussen (Ed.), *Carmichael's manual of child psychology* (Vol. II, 3rd ed.). New York: John Wiley.

Hepler, J. B., & Rose, S. D. (1988). Evaluation of a multi-component group approach for improving the social skills of elementary school children. *Journal of Social Service Research, 11,* 1-18.

Hess, A. M., Rosenberg, M. S., & Levy, G. K. (1990). Reducing truancy in students with mild handicaps. *Remedial and Special Education, 11,* 14-28.

Hetherington, E. M. (1979). Divorce: A child's perspective. *American Psychologist, 34,* 851-858.

Hetherington, E. M., Cox, M., & Cox, R. (1982). Effects of divorce on parents and children. In M. E. Lamb (Ed.), *Nontraditional families: Parenting and child development* (pp. 233-288). Hillsdale, NJ: Lawrence Erlbaum.

Hett, G. G., & Rose, C. D. (1991). Counselling children of divorce: A divorce lifeline program. *Canadian Journal of Counselling, 25,* 38-49.

Hoffman, C. E. (1984). Group session in a middle school. *Children Today, 13,* 25-26.

Hogan, P. T., Schaffer, D., & Villanueva, S. (1982). The use of photography as an intervention technique with physically disabled adolescents. *School Social Work Journal, 6,* 100-104.

Holmes, W. D., & Wagner, K. D. (1992). Psychotherapy treatments for depression in children and adolescents. *Journal of Psychotherapy Practice and Research, 1,* 313-323.

Homes, T. H., & Rahe, R. H. (1967). The social readjustment scale. *Journal of Psychosomatic Research, 11,* 213-218.

Hoyt, L. A., Cowen, E. L., Pedro-Carroll, J. L., & Alpert-Gillis, L. J. (1990). Anxiety and depression in young children of divorce. *Journal of Clinical Child Psychology, 19,* 26-32.

Hudson, W. W. (1992). *The WALMYR assessment scales scoring manual.* Tempe, AZ: WALMYR Publishing Company.

Huey, W. C. (1983). Reducing adolescent aggression through group assertive training. *School Counselor, 30,* 193-202.

Hugill, S., Hindmarch, C., Woolford, A., & Austen, H. (1987). Prevention is better than referral. *Support for Learning, 2,* 27-35.

Jaffe, S. L., & Kalman, B. (1991). Group therapy. In J. M. Weiner (Ed.), *Textbook of child and adolescent psychiatry.* Washington, DC: American Psychiatric Press.

Jenkins, P. H. (1995). School delinquency and school commitment. *Sociology of Education, 68,* 221-239.

Johnson, C., & Connors, M. (1987). *The etiology and treatment of bulimia nervosa.* New York: Basic Books.

Johnson, K. (1989). *Trauma in the lives of children.* Alameda, CA: Hunter House.

Johnson, K. (1992). *School crisis management.* Almeda, CA: Hunter House.

Kalter, N., Pickar, J., & Lesowitz, M. (1984). School-based developmental facilitation groups for children of divorce: A preventive intervention. *American Journal of Orthopsychiatry, 54,* 613-623.

Kalter, N., Schaefer, M., Lesowitz, M., Alpern, D., & Pickar, J. (1988). School-based support groups for children of divorce. In B. H. Gottlieb (Ed.), *Marshaling social support: Formats, processes, and effects* (pp. 165-185). Newbury Park, CA: Sage.

Kalter, N., & Schreier, S. (1994). Developmental facilitation groups for children of divorce: The elementary school model. In C. W. LeCroy (Ed.), *Handbook of child and adolescent treatment manuals* (pp. 307-342). New York: Lexington Books.

Kanoy, K. W., & Cunningham, J. L. (1984). Consensus of confusion in research on children and divorce: Conceptual and methodological issues. *Journal of Divorce, 7,* 45-71.

Kazdin, A. E., French, N. H., Unis, A. S., Esveldt-Dawson, K., & Sherick, R. B. (1983). Hopelessness, depression, and suicidal intent among psychiatrically disturbed children. *Journal of Consulting and Clinical Psychology, 51,* 504-510.

Kelly, J. B., & Wallerstein, J. S. (1979). Children of divorce. *The National Elementary Principal, 59,* 51-58.

Kendall, P. C., Kortlander, E., Chansky, T. E., & Brady, E. U. (1992). Comorbidity of anxiety and depression in youth: Treatment implications. *Journal of Consulting and Clinical Psychology, 60,* 869-880.

Kennedy, J. F. (1989). The heterogeneous group for chronically physically ill and physically healthy but emotionally disturbed children and adolescents. *International Journal of Group Psychotherapy, 39,* 105-125.

Kiresuk, T. J., & Sherman, R. E. (1968). Goal attainment scaling: A general method for evaluating comprehensive mental health programs. *Community Mental Health Journal, 4,* 443-453.

Kiresuk, T. J., & Sherman, R. E. (1977). A reply to the critique of goal attainment scaling. *Social Work Research & Abstracts, 13,* 9-11.

Kirsch, I. S., Jungeblut, A., Jenkins, L., & Kolstad, A. (1993). *Adult literacy in America: A first look at the results of the National Adult Literacy Survey.* Washington, DC: U.S. Government Printing Office.

Kochendofer, S. A., & Culp, D. (1979). Relaxation group-intake procedure. *Elementary School Guidance & Counseling, 14,* 124.

Kohlberg, L., LaCrosse, J., & Ricks, D. (1972). The predictability of adult mental health from childhood behavior. In B. B. Wolman (Ed.), *Manual of child psychopathology* (pp. 1217-1284). New York: McGraw-Hill.

Kohn, M., & Claussen, J. (1955). Social isolation and schizophrenia. *American Sociological Review, 20,* 265-273.

Kostoulas, K. H., Berkovitz, I. H., & Arima, H. (1991). School counseling groups and children of divorce: Loosening attachment to mother in adolescent groups. *Journal of Child and Adolescent Group Therapy, 1,* 177-192.

Kovnat, R. (1979). Classroom discussion groups. *School Social Work Journal, 4,* 30-34.

Kurdek, L. A. (1987). Children's adjustment to parental divorce: An ecological perspective. In J. P. Vincent (Ed.), *Advances in family intervention, assessment and theory* (Vol. 4, pp. 1-31). Greenwich, CT: JAI.

Kurdek, L. A. (1988). Social support of divorced single mothers and their children. *Journal of Divorce, 11,* 167-187.

Kurdek, L. A., & Berg, B. (1987). Children's Beliefs About Parental Divorce Scale: Psychometric characteristics and concurrent validity. *Journal of Consulting and Clinical Psychology, 55,* 712-718.

LaGreca, A. M., & Santogrossi, D. A. (1980). Social skills training with elementary school students: A behavioral group approach. *Journal of Consulting and Clinical Psychology, 48,* 220-227.

LeCoq, L. L., & Capuzzi, D. (1984). Preventing adolescent drug abuse. *Journal of Humanistic Education and Development, 22,* 155-169.

LeCroy, C. W. (1986). An analysis of the effects of gender on outcome in group treatment with young adolescents. *Journal of Youth & Adolescence, 15,* 497-508.

LeCroy, C. (1987). Teaching children social skills: A game format. *Social Work, 32,* 440-442.

LeCroy, C. W. (1992). Enhancing the delivery of effective mental health services to children. *Social Work, 37,* 225-231.

LeCroy, C. W., & Rose, S. D. (1986). Evaluation of preventive interventions for enhancing social competence in adolescents. *Social Work Research & Abstracts, 22,* 8-16.

LeCroy, C., & Rose, S. R. (1986). Helping children cope with stress. *Social Work in Education, 9,* 5-15.

Lee, D. Y., Hallberg, E. T., Slemon, A. G., & Haase, R. F. (1985). An assertiveness scale for adolescents. *Journal of Clinical Psychology, 41,* 51-57.

Leone, S. D., & Gumaer, J. (1979). Group assertiveness training of shy children. *The School Counselor, 27,* 134-141.

Lesowitz, M., Kalter, N., Pickar, J., Chethik, & Schaefer, M. (1987). School-based developmental facilitation groups for children of divorce: Issues of group process. *Psychotherapy, 24,* 90-95.

Livesley, W. J., & Bromley, D. B. (1973). *Person perception in childhood and adolescence.* New York: John Wiley.

Lokken, M. (1982). Three group guidance methods that work. *Elementary School Guidance and Counseling, 17,* 142-149.

Lopez, J. (1991). Group work as a protective factor for immigrant youth. *Social Work With Groups, 14,* 29-42.

Lovins, J. H., & Bogal, R. B. (1980). Role play: A tool for handling interpersonal conflict in the classroom. *School Social Work Journal, 5,* 4-10.

Lufi, D., & Cohen, A. (1987). A scale for measuring persistence in children. *Journal of Personality Assessment, 51,* 178-185.

Marsh, H. W. (1993). Academic self-concept: Theory measurement and research. In J. Suls (Ed.), *Psychological perspectives on the self* (Vol. 45, pp. 59-98). Hillsdale, NJ: Lawrence Erlbaum.

Marsh, H. W., Chessor, D., Craven, R., & Roche, L. (1995). The effects of gifted and talented programs on academic self-concept: The big fish strikes again. *American Educational Research Journal, 32,* 285-319.

McCubbin, H. I., & Thompson, A. I. (Eds.). (1991). *Family assessment inventories for research and practice.* Madison: University of Wisconsin Press.

McCullagh, J. G. (1981). The art of saying no: Group assertion training with seventh grade students. *School Social Work Journal, 6,* 7-18.

McWhinney, M., Haskins-Herkenham, D., & Hare, I. (1991). *NASW Commission on Education Position Statement: The School Social Worker and Confidentiality.* Silver Spring, MD: National Association of Social Workers.

Meares, P. (1980). Interrupted time series design and the evaluation of school practice. *Social Work in Education, 2,* 51-52.

Mervis, B. A. (1989). Shaggy dog stories: A video project for children of divorce. *Social Work in Education, 12,* 16-26.

Midgley, C., Anderman, E., & Hicks, L. (1995). Differences between elementary and middle school teachers and students: A goal theory approach. *Journal of Early Adolescence, 15,* 90-113.

Miller, L. C. (1972). School behavior check list: An inventory of deviant behavior for elementary school children. *Journal of Consulting and Clinical Psychology, 38,* 134-144.

Miller, N., & Gentry, K. W. (1980). Sociometric indices of children's peer interaction in the school setting. In H. C. Foot, A. J. Chapman, & J. R. Smith (Eds.), *Friendship and social relations in children* (pp. 145-177). Chichester, UK: Wiley.

Mitchell, J. (1983). When disaster strikes: The critical incident stress debriefing process. *Journal of Emergency Medical Services, 8,* 36-39.

Moore, P. (1995). Information problem solving: A wider view of library skills. *Contemporary Educational Psychology, 20,* 1-31.

Moore, S. G. (1967). Correlates of peer acceptance in nursery school children. In W. W. Hartup & N. L. Smothergill (Eds.), *The young child.* Washington, DC: National Association for the Education of Young Children.

Morse, B. A., Bartolotta, C. N., Cushman, L. G., & Rubin, P. T. (1982). "End-of-term blues": An annual dilemma. *Social Work in Education, 5,* 26-40.

Moss, W. L. (1992). Group psychotherapy with adolescents in a residential treatment center. *Journal of Child and Adolescent Group Therapy, 2,* 93-104.

Mueller, C. W. (1993). Attention-deficit hyperactivity disorder and school social work practice. *Social Work in Education, 15,* 104-112.

Munsch, J., & Kinchen, K. M. (1995). Adolescent sociometric status and social support. *Journal of Early Adolescence, 15,* 181-202.

Myrick, R. D., & Dixon, R. W. (1985). Changing student attitudes and behavior through group counseling. *School Counselor, 32,* 325-330.

National Center for Health Statistics (1990). Advance report of final divorce statistics, 1987. *Monthly Vital Statistics Report* (Vol. 38, no. 12, supp. 2). Hyattsville, MD: U.S. Public Health Service.

National Council of State Consultants for School Social Work Services (1981). Staffing needs for providing school social work services to pupils. *School Social Work Journal, 6,* 45-50.

Neugebauer, R. (1989). Divorce, custody, and visitation: The child's point of view. *Journal of Divorce, 13,* 153-167.

Newman, R. S. (1991). Goals and self-regulated learning: What motivates children to seek academic help? In M. L. Maehr & P. R. Pintrich (Eds.), *Advances in motivation and achievement* (Vol. 7, pp. 151-183). Greenwich, CT: JAI.

Newman, R. S., & Schwager, M. T. (1995). Students' help seeking during problem solving: Effects of grade, goal, and prior achievement. *American Educational Research Journal, 32,* 352-376.

Newton-Logsdon, G., & Armstrong, M. I. (1993). School-based mental health services. *Social Work in Education, 15,* 187-191.

Ollendick, T. H., & Francis, G. (1988). Behavioral assessment and treatment of childhood phobias. *Behavior Modification, 12,* 165-204.

Omizo, M. M., & Omizo, S. A. (1987). Group counseling with children of divorce: New findings. *Elementary School Guidance & Counseling, 22,* 46-52.

Omizo, M. M., & Omizo, S. A. (1988). The effects of participation in group counseling sessions on self-esteem and locus of control among adolescents from divorced families. *The School Counselor, 36,* 54-60.

Oppawsky, J. (1991). Utilizing children's drawings in working with children following divorce. *Journal of Divorce and Remarriage, 15,* 125-141.

Owen, M. C., & Sabatino, C. A. (1989). Effects of cognitive development on classroom behavior: A model assessment and intervention program. *Social Work in Education, 11,* 77-87.

Parsons, R. J. (1988). Empowerment for role alternatives for low income minority girls: A group work approach. *Social Work With Groups, 11,* 27-45.

Pasternack, R., & Peres, Y. (1990). To what extent can the school reduce the gaps between children raised by divorced and intact families? *Journal of Divorce and Remarriage, 15,* 143-157.

Pedro-Carroll, J. L., Alpert-Gillis, L. J., & Cowen, E. L. (1992). An evaluation of the efficacy of a preventive intervention for 4th-6th grade urban children of divorce. *The Journal of Primary Prevention, 13,* 115-130.

Pedro-Carroll, J. L., & Cowen, E. L. (1985). The children of divorce intervention program: An investigation of the efficacy of a school-based prevention program. *Journal of Consulting and Clinical Psychology, 53,* 603-611.

Pedro-Carroll, J. L., Cowen, E. L., & Gillis, L. (1989). The children of divorce intervention program. *Journal of Consulting and Clinical Psychology, 57,* 583-588.

Pedro-Carroll, J. L., Cowen, E. L., Hightower, A. D., & Guare, J. C. (1986). Preventive intervention with latency-aged children of divorce: A replication study. *American Journal of Community Psychology, 14,* 277-290.

Pfeifer, G., & Abrams, L. (1984). School-based discussion groups for children of divorce: A pilot program. *Group, 8,* 22-28.

Pines, M. (1982, April 19). Divorce: Children follow in parents' footsteps. *Chicago Tribune.*

Platt, J. J. Spivack, G., Altman, N., Altman, D., & Piezzer, S. B. (1974). Adolescent problem-solving thinking. *Journal of Consulting & Clinical Psychology, 42,* 787-793.

Platt, J. J., Spivack, G., & Bloom, M. (1971). *Means-ends problem-solving procedure (MEPS): Manual and tentative norms.* Philadelphia: Hahnenmann Medical College and Hospital.

Pollak, J., & Schaffer, S. (1984). Group boundary maintenance and the alternative high school. *Social Work in Education, 7,* 35-48.

Pope, L. A., Campbell, M., & Kurtz, P. D. (1992). Hostage crisis: A school-based interdisciplinary approach to posttraumatic stress disorder. *Social Work in Education, 14,* 227-233.

Praport, H. (1993). Reducing high school attrition: Group counseling can help. *The School Counselor, 40,* 309-311.

Prokop, M. S. (1990). Children of divorce: Relearning happiness. *Momentum, 21,* 72-73.

Pumfrey, P. D., & Ward, J. (1976). Adjustment from primary to secondary school. *Educational Research, 19,* 25-34.

Quay, H. C., & Peterson, D. R. (1983). *Revised Behavior Problem Checklist.* Coral Gables, FL: University of Miami Press.

Ranbom, S. (1986). *School dropouts: Everybody's problem.* Washington, DC: Institute for Educational Leadership.

Randolph, A. H. (1982). Group processes for classroom teachers. In F. B. Meadows, Jr., F. H. Wallbrown, & L. Litwack (Eds.), *Using guidance skills in the classroom* (pp. 184-203). Springfield, IL: Charles C Thomas.

Rauch, S. P., Brack, C. J., & Orr, D. P. (1987). School-based, short-term group treatment for behaviorally disturbed young adolescent males: A pilot intervention. *Journal of School Health, 57,* 19-22.

Richert, A. J. (1986). An experiential group treatment for behavioral disorders. *Techniques: A Journal for Remedial Education and Counseling, 2,* 249-255.

Rodgers, D. C. (1980). Stepping-up school attendance. *National Association of Secondary School Principals Bulletin, 64,* 122-124.

Roe, V. (1993). An interactive therapy group. *Child Language Teaching and Therapy, 9,* 133-140.

Roff, M. (1961). Childhood social interactions and young adult bad conduct. *Journal of Abnormal Social Psychology, 63,* 333-337.

Roff, M., Sells, S. B., & Golden, M. M. (1972). *Social adjustment and personality development in children.* Minneapolis: University of Minnesota Press.

Rogers, K. T., Segal, E. A., & Graham, M. (1994). The relationship between academic factors and running away among adolescents. *Social Work in Education, 16,* 46-54.

Rohde, R. I., & Stockton, R. (1993). The group as an effective medium for working with children of chemically dependent families. *The Journal for Specialists in Group Work, 18,* 182-188.

Rooney, R. (1977). Adolescent groups in public schools. In W. J. Reid & L. Epstein (Eds.), *Task-centered practice* (pp. 168-182). New York: Columbia University Press.

Rose, S. R. (1985). Development of children's social competence in classroom groups. *Social Work in Education, 8,* 48-58.

Rose, S. R. (1986). Enhancing the social relationship skills of children: A comparative study of group approaches. *School Social Work Journal, 10,* 76-85.

Rose, S. R., & Downs, W. R. (1989). Adolescent social groups: Peer perceptions, attitudes, and activities. *Social Work in Education, 12,* 27-44.

Ross, A. O., Lacey, H. M., & Parton, D. A. (1965). The development of a behavior checklist for boys. *Child Development, 36,* 1013-1027.

Ross, S., & Bilson, A. (1981). The sunshine group: An example of social work intervention through the use of a group. *Social Work With Groups, 4,* 15-28.

Rubin, K. H., & Pepler, D. J. (1980). The relationship of child's play to social-cognitive growth and development. In H. C. Foot, A. J. Chapman, & J. R. Smith (Eds.), *Friendship and social relations in children* (pp. 209-233). Chichester, UK: Wiley.

Sarason, I. G., & Sarason, B. R. (1981). Teaching cognitive and social skills to high school students. *Journal of Consulting and Clinical Psychology, 49,* 908-918.

Schechtman, Z. (1993). School adjustment and small-group therapy: An Israeli study. *Journal of Counseling & Development, 72,* 77-81.

Scheidlinger, S. (1985). Group treatment of adolescents: An overview. *American Journal of Orthopsychiatry, 55,* 102-111.

Schiffer, M. (1983). S. R. Slavson (1890-1981). *International Journal of Group Psychotherapy, 33,* 131-150.

Schnedeker, J. A. (1991). Multistage group guidance and counseling for low-achieving students. *The School Counselor, 39,* 47-51.

Schreier, S., & Kalter, N. (1990). School-based developmental facilitation groups for children of divorce. *Social Work in Education, 13,* 58-67.

Schwartz, W. (1961). The social worker in the group. In National Conference on Social Welfare (Ed.), *New perspectives on services to groups: Theory, organization, and practice* (pp. 7-34). New York: National Association of Social Workers.

Schwartz, W. (1971). On the use of groups in social work practice. In W. Schwartz & S. Zalba (Eds.), *The practice of group work* (pp. 3-24). New York: Columbia University Press.

Schwebel, R. (1992). Support groups for adolescents. *Alcohol & Other Drugs Review, 1,* 2-3.

Scott, R. T. (1994). Dealing with the aftermath of a crisis, trauma and disaster: An overview of intervention strategies for children. *The Child, Youth, and Family Services Quarterly, 17,* 6-10.

Shantz, C. U. (1975). The development of social cognition. In E. M. Hetherington (Ed.), *Review of child development research* (Vol. 5). Chicago: University of Chicago Press.

Shantz, C. U. (1983). Social cognition. In J. H. Flavell & E. M. Markman (Eds.), *Handbook of child psychology* (Vol. 3, pp. 495-555). New York: John Wiley.

Shelby, J. (1994). Psychological intervention with children in disaster relief shelters. *The Child, Youth, and Family Services Quarterly, 17,* 14-18.

Sherborne, V. (1990). *Developmental movement for children.* Cambridge, UK: Cambridge University Press.

Shields, S. A. (1985). Busted and branded: Group work with substance abusing adolescents in schools. *Social Work With Groups, 8,* 61-81.

Shinar, D. (1983). Television production as content and process in social work with groups: An experiment with disadvantaged neighborhood youth in Israel. *Social Work With Groups, 6,* 23-25.

Shorey, A. E. (1981). Peer counseling and achievement motivation: A comparison of two counseling approaches in an urban middle school (Doctoral dissertation, Northwestern University, 1981). *Dissertation Abstracts International, 42,* 1966-A.

Shure, M. B., & Spivack, G. (1972). Means-ends thinking, adjustment, and social class among elementary-school-aged children. *Journal of Consulting and Clinical Psychology, 38,* 348-353.

Shwalb, D. W., Shwalb, B. J., & Nakazawa, J. (1995). Competitive and cooperative attitudes: A longitudinal survey of Japanese adolescents. *Journal of Early Adolescence, 15,* 145-168.

Simmons, R. G., Blythe, D., Van Cleave, E., & Bush, D. (1979). Entry into early adolescence: Impact of school structure, puberty, and early dating on self-esteem. *American Sociological Review, 44,* 948-967.

Singleton, L. C., & Asher, S. R. (1977). Peer preferences and social interaction among third-grade children in an integrated school district. *Journal of Educational Psychology, 69,* 330-336.

Slavson, S. R., & Schiffer, M. (1975). *Group psychotherapies for children: A textbook.* New York: International Universities Press.

Somers, M. L. (1976). Problem-solving in small groups. In R. W. Roberts & H. Northen (Eds.), *Theories of social work with groups* (pp. 331-367). New York: Columbia University Press.

Sonnenshein-Schneider, M., & Baird, K. L. (1980). Group counseling children of divorce in the elementary schools: Understanding process and technique. *Personnel and Guidance Journal, 59,* 88-91.

Spivack, G., & Levine, M. (1973). *Self-regulation in acting out and normal adolescents* (Report M-4531). Washington, DC: National Institutes of Health.

Spivack, G., Platt, J. J., & Shure, M. B. (1976). *The problem solving approach to adjustment.* San Francisco: Jossey-Bass.

Spivack, G., & Shure, M. B. (1974). *Social adjustment of young children: A cognitive approach to solving real-life problems.* San Francisco: Jossey-Bass.

REFERENCES 175

Sprang, B. P. (1989). Developmental issues in assessing chemical dependence. *Student Assistance Journal, 2,* 15-22.

Stark, K. D., Rouse, L. W., & Livingston, R. (1991). Treatment of depression during childhood and adolescence: Cognitive-behavioral procedures for the individual and the family. In P. C. Kendall (Ed.), *Child and adolescent therapy: Cognitive-behavioral approaches* (pp. 165-198). New York: Guilford.

Staudt, M. M., & Craft, J. L. (1983). School staff input in the evaluation of school social work practice. *Social Work in Education, 5,* 119-131.

Stengel, B. E. (1987). Developmental group therapy with autistic and other severely psychosocially handicapped adolescents. *International Journal of Group Psychotherapy, 37,* 417-431.

Stevenson, R. G. (1986). The child and suffering: The role of the school. *Loss, Grief & Care, 1,* 151-153.

Stillion, J. M., McDowell, E. E., & May, J. H. (1989). *Suicide across the life span: Premature exits.* New York: Hemisphere Publishing.

Stolberg, A. L., & Garrison, K. M. (1985). Evaluating a primary prevention program for children of divorce. *American Journal of Community Psychology, 13,* 111-124.

Stolberg, A. L., & Mahler, J. L. (1989). Protecting children from the consequences of divorce: An empirically derived approach. *Prevention in Human Services, 7,* 161-176.

Strauss, J. B., & McGann, J. (1987). Building a network for children of divorce. *Social Work in Education, 9,* 96-105.

Stumphauzer, J. S. (1980). Behavioral analysis questionnaire for adolescent drinkers. *Psychological Reports, 47,* 641-642.

Tannenbaum, J. (1990). An English conversation group model for Vietnamese adolescent females. *Social Work With Groups, 13,* 41-55.

Tedder, S. L., Scherman, A., & Wantz, R. A. (1987). Effectiveness of a support group for children of divorce. *Elementary School Guidance & Counseling, 22,* 102-109.

Thoma, E. (1964). Group psychotherapy with underachieving girls in a public high school. *Journal of Individual Psychology, 20,* 96-100.

Timberlake, E. M., & Sabatino, C. A. (1994). Homeless children: Impact of school attendance on self-esteem and loneliness. *Social Work in Education, 16,* 9-20.

Timmer, D. F. (1995). Group support for teenagers with attention deficit hyperactivity disorder. *Social Work in Education, 17,* 194-198.

Toepfer, C., & Marani, J. (1980). School based research. In M. Johnson (Ed.), *Toward adolescence: The middle school years. Seventy-ninth yearbook of the National Society for the Study of Education.* Chicago: University of Chicago Press.

Toro, P. (1984). *Social problem solving skills and school behavior of learning disabled children.* Paper presented at the meeting of the American Psychological Association, Toronto, Canada. (ERIC Document Reproduction Service No. ED 258 373)

Trautman, P. D., & Shaffer, D. (1984). Treatment of children and adolescent suicide attempters. In H. S. Sudak, A. B. Ford, & N. B. Rushford (Eds.), *Suicide in the young.* Boston: John Wright.

Treffinger, D. J. (1995). Creative problem solving: Overview and educational implications. *Educational Psychology Review, 7,* 301-312.

Ullmann, C. A. (1957). Teachers, peers, and tests as predictors of adjustment. *Journal of Educational Psychology, 48,* 257-267.

Urdan, T. C., & Maehr, M. L. (1995). Beyond a two-goal theory of motivation and achievement: A case for social goals. *Review of Educational Research, 65,* 213-243.

Vandell, D. L., & Mueller, E. C. (1980). Peer play and friendships during the first two years. In H. C. Foot, A. J. Chapman, & J. R. Smith (Eds.), *Friendship and social relations in children* (pp. 181-208). Chichester, UK: Wiley.

Vinter, R. (1985). Program activities: An analysis of their effects on participant behaviour. In M. Sundel, P. Glasser, R. Sarri, & R. Vinter (Eds.). *Individual change through small groups* (2nd ed., pp. 226-236). New York: Free Press.

Vogel, J., & Vernberg, E. M. (1993). Children's psychological responses to disaster. *Journal of Clinical Child Psychology, 22,* 464-484.

Wallerstein, J. S., & Kelly, J. B. (1976). The effects of parental divorce: Experiences of the child in later latency. *American Journal of Orthopsychiatry, 46,* 256-269.

Wallerstein, J. S., & Kelly, J. B. (1980). *Surviving the breakup: How children and parents cope with divorce.* New York: Basic Books.

Walsh, R. T., Richardson, M. A., & Cardey, R. M. (1991). Structured fantasy approaches to children's group therapy. *Social Work With Groups, 14,* 57-73.

Walter, J., & Peters, R. D. (1980). *Social problem solving in aggressive elementary school boys.* Paper presented at the meeting of the Canadian Psychological Association, Alberta, Canada.

Watt, N. F. (1979). The longitudinal research base for early intervention. *Journal of Community Psychology, 7,* 158-168.

Webb, N. B. (Ed.). (1993). *Helping bereaved children: A handbook for practitioners.* New York: Guilford.

Welsh, B. L. (1984). Preparation programs for school practice. *Social Work in Education, 6,* 279-284.

West, M., Carlin, M., Baserman, B., & Milstein, M. (1978). An intensive therapeutic program for learning disabled prepubertal children. *Journal of Learning Disabilities, 11,* 56-59.

Wiener, L. S., Spencer, E. D., Davidson, R., & Fair, C. (1993). National telephone support groups: A new avenue toward psychosocial support for HIV-infected children and their families. *Social Work With Groups, 16,* 55-71.

Wiggins, J. D., & Moody, A. H. (1987). Student evaluations of counseling programs: An added dimension. *The School Counselor, 34,* 353-361.

Wiggins, J. D., & Wiggins, M. M. (1992). Elementary students' self-esteem and behavioral ratings related to counselor time-task emphases. *The School Counselor, 39,* 377-381.

Williams, M. B. (1984). Family dissolution: An issue for the schools: An elementary school program. *Children Today, 13,* 25-26.

Windle, M., Miller-Tutzauer, C., Barnes, G. M., & Welte, J. (1991). Adolescent perceptions of help-seeking resources for substance abuse. *Child Development, 62,* 179-189.

Witkin, S. L., Shapiro, C. H., & McCall, M. (1980). How to evaluate public welfare training. *Public Welfare, 38,* 25-35.

Wodarski, J. S. (1988). Preventive health services for adolescents: A practice paradigm. *Social Work in Education, 11,* 5-20.

Womersley, S. (1993). Reflections upon techniques used in a school-based groupwork programme. *Therapeutic Care and Education, 2,* 222-242.

Yeast, C. (1994). APA disaster response network: Psychological response to survivors of traumatic events. *The Child, Youth, and Family Services Quarterly, 17,* 19-20.

Zinner, E. S. (1987). Responding to suicide in schools: A case study in loss intervention and group survivorship. *Journal of Counseling and Development, 65,* 499-501.

INDEX

ABOUT THE AUTHOR

Steven R. Rose is Professor of Social Work at Louisiana State University. He received the MSW from Washington University (St. Louis) and the PhD from the University of Wisconsin, in Madison. He has served as a faculty member at the Hebrew University of Jerusalem and the University of Vermont, and as a visiting faculty member at Bar-Ilan University. He has held professional positions in schools and in mental health and child, youth, and family agencies. He conducts research on social services for children and adolescents.